D1599829

An Annotated Critical Bibliography of George Eliot

An Annotated Critical Bibliography of George Eliot

George Levine
Professor of English, Rutgers University

With the assistance of Patricia O'Hara

St. Martin's Press
New York

All rights reserved. For information, write:
Scholarly and Reference Division,
St. Martin's Press, Inc., 175 Fifth Avenue, New York, NY 10010

First published in the United States of America in 1988

Printed in Great Britain

ISBN 0-312-01959-9

Library of Congress Cataloging-in-Publication Data

Levine, George Lewis.
 An annotated critical bibliography of George Eliot
with the assistance of Patricia O'Hara.

 Includes index.
 1. Eliot, George, 1819–1880—Bibliography. I. O'Hara,
Patricia. II. Title.
Z8259.L48 1988 [PR4681] 016.823'8 88-3044
ISBN 0-312-01959-9

For Allon White
The most vital of scholars, critics, friends
with love

Contents

Advice to the Reader

In recent years, George Eliot has attracted an enormous amount of critical attention. The revival of interest in her became evident just after the Second World War and was marked by F.R. Leavis's inclusion of her in his rather exclusive "Great Tradition". In the mid- and late 1950s, critics and scholars like Barbara Hardy began to find in her work a kind of formal brilliance that was akin to if still rather different from the Jamesian formalism that at the time was dominating criticism. Since then, George Eliot has been studied from almost every conceivable intellectual direction. The philosophical and moral substance of her novels, which were partly responsible for the decline in her reputation among all things Victorian at the turn of the century, has been reconsidered, and the extraordinary power of her intelligence has won renewed respect. The most recent critical developments have found fertile ground in her narratives, as witness the deconstructive essays of J. Hillis Miller and Cynthia Chase. Moreover, since the development of a serious modern feminist criticism, her works and her life have been studied, analysed, criticized in new ways, and seem to provide endless resources for further study.

Given the vastness of the Bibliography that has developed over the past forty years, it would be impossible and unwise to attempt to achieve full coverage of all works about her. This Bibliography is, after all, 'critical', and judgements have had to be made at every step. It carries GE scholarship through 1984, and in a very few instances includes later work—up to 1986— of very great importance which I have had the chance to read before this Bibliography went to press. It lists, of course, many essays and volumes with which I disagree or whose arguments I do not find helpful. But all listings are intended to give a sense of the fundamental arguments about GE, the fundamental facts gathered by scholars through the years. The Bibliography does include many 'minor' pieces, in part because they too can be interesting, but in part also to provide the flavour of much of the criticism and scholarship that I have been forced to exclude. In principle, I have tried to exclude entries for essays that have later appeared in books. With all its inevitable limitations and omissions, this Bibliography should provide an overview of the main trends in George Eliot criticism and should open access to fuller bibliographical information, if the reader desires it.

Obviously, some of the categories under which items are listed are arbitrarily defined. In cases where an item seems peculiarly appropriate to more than one category, the other is noted in parentheses at the end of the entry.

Within each category, entries are arranged in chronological order, and alphabetically within particular years.

George Levine

Acknowledgements

Bibliographies are difficult things to construct, particularly if they are constructed alone. In the first stages of this one, I was helped enormously by Jane Kenney, who did a great deal of leg and head work to supplement the initial bibliography I had myself compiled over the years. But the completion of this work was only possible because of the assistance of Patricia O'Hara, who not only completed the supplementary work that Jane Kenney had begun, but who found the photocopies and inter-library loan copies of texts hard of access. Indeed, she became as much co-author as assistant, for many of the annotations in this final version are her own, and much of what was wrong with my own annotations has been excised because of her careful editorial eye.

Bibliographical Tools

(Thorough annual bibliographies are included in the "Victorian Bibliography" published each year in *Victorian Studies,* and in the annual bibliography of the Modern Language Association published in *PMLA.*)

1 Harvey, W.J.
"George Eliot", in VICTORIAN FICTION: A GUIDE TO RESEARCH, ed. Lionel Stevenson (Cambridge, Mass: Harvard University Press, 1964), pp. 294-323

An excellent overview—with evaluative descriptions and listings— of George Eliot studies up to 1964.

2 Marshall, William H.
"A Selective Bibliography of Writings about George Eliot to 1965", *Bulletin of Bibliography,* 25 (1967), 70-2, 88-94

As the title indicates, a selective bibliography. Its usefulness is diminished by the fact that books and articles are not listed separately and are presented in strictly alphabetical, not chronological order.

3 Beaty, Jerome
"George Eliot", THE ENGLISH NOVEL: SELECT BIBLIOGRAPHICAL GUIDES, ed. A.E. Dyson (London: Oxford University Press, 1974), pp. 246-63

A very useful survey and evaluation of the critical tradition.

4 Fulmer, Constance Marie
GEORGE ELIOT: A REFERENCE GUIDE (Boston: G.K. Hall, 1977)

The most complete GE bibliography to its date, covering almost every item about her from 1858 to 1971, and including some light annotation.

5 Knoepflmacher, U.C.

"George Eliot", in VICTORIAN FICTION: A SECOND GUIDE TO RESEARCH, ed. George Ford (New York: Modern Language Association of America, 1978), pp. 234-73

Brings Harvey's survey up to 1978.

6   Higdon, David Leon
"A Bibliography of George Eliot Criticism 1971-1977", *Bulletin of Bibliography,* 37 (1980), 90-103

A continuation of Marshall's bibliography.

Primary Materials

(See also Collins in 49; Baker in 50)

7   Kitchel, Anna (ed.)
QUARRY FOR MIDDLEMARCH (Berkeley: University of California Press, 1950), supplement to *Nineteenth-Century Fiction,* 1950

A Notebook GE used in preparation for *Middlemarch.* Notes on science are backed by notes on the novel's structure.

8   Dodd, Valerie A. (ed.)
"A George Eliot Notebook", *Studies in Bibliography* (1981), 258-62

Describes a 42-leaf notebook in the Nuneaton Library entitled "Greek Philosophy & Locke & Comte", compiled after *Daniel Deronda.*

9   Haight, Gordon S. (ed.)
THE GEORGE ELIOT LETTERS, 7 vols (New Haven. Conn.: Yale University Press, 1954, 1955)

The publication of these letters marked a turning-point in the study of George Eliot, making available masses of new material in totally reliable form. These letters form the basis of Haight's own definitive biography of GE and of almost all serious work on her life and the development of her art. The first three volumes were published in 1954, the last four in 1955.

10   Beaty, Jerome
"George Eliot's Notebook for an Unwritten Novel", *Princeton University Library Chronicle,* 18 (1957), 175-82

A description of GE's plans for what would have been her last novel.

11   Paris, Bernard
"George Eliot's Unpublished Poetry", *Studies in Philology,* 56 (1959), 539-58

Prints "In a London Drawing Room", "Ex Oriente Lux", "In the South", and some fragments.

(POETRY)

3

12   Haight, Gordon S.
        "The George Eliot and George Henry Lewes Collection", *Yale University Library Gazette,* 35 (1961), 170-1

        A description of the collection that holds most of GE's journals and diaries.

13   Pinney, Thomas
        ESSAYS OF GEORGE ELIOT (New York: Columbia University Press; London: Routledge & Kegan Paul, 1963)

        Standard collection of the most important of GE's essays and notes, well introduced and annotated.

                                                    (CRITICAL WRITING)

14   Pinney, Thomas
        "More Leaves from George Eliot's Notebook", *Huntington Library Quarterly,* 29 (1966), 353-76

        Pages omitted from the publication by Lewes's son of "Leaves from a Notebook".

15   Baker, William
        "George Eliot's Projected Napoleonic War Novel: an Unnoted Reading List", *Nineteenth-Century Fiction,* 29 (1975), 453-60

        Describes the reading list that makes part of the quarry for the unwritten novel described in Beaty (10). The list appears on the back of two of the folio sheets. Shows that her interests were "narrowing to the Napoleonic War period, including the issues of law reform, military developments, religious freedom in Ireland, the problems of depressed populations."

16   Baker, William
        SOME GEORGE ELIOT NOTEBOOKS: AN EDITION OF THE CARL H. PFORZHEIMER LIBRARY'S GEORGE ELIOT HOLOGRAPH NOTEBOOKS, 707, 708, 709, 710, 711 (Salzburg: Institut für Englische Sprache und Literatur, University of Salzburg: vol. 1, MS 707, 1976; vol. 2, MS 708, 1984; vol. 3, MS 711, 1980; vol. 4, MSS 709, 710, 1985)

        A transcription with notes of the Pforzheimer notebooks. Vol. 4 contains a useful list of GE's reading materials cited in the five notebooks.

17   Baker, William
      THE GEORGE ELIOT–GEORGE HENRY LEWES
      LIBRARY: AN ANNOTATED CATALOGUE OF THEIR
      BOOKS AT DR WILLIAMS'S LIBRARY, LONDON (New
      York: Garland Publishing, 1977)

      A description of the library of Dr Williams, to whom Lewes's
      son gave almost all of the philosphical and scientific works from
      his father's library. A very careful and extensive analysis of the
      books read by Lewes and GE, the "Introduction" is a resource
      for future scholarship on them.

18   Chapman, Raymond and Gottlieb, Eleanora
      "A Russian View of George Eliot", *Nineteenth-Century
      Fiction*, 33 (1978), 348-65

      A translation of an article, written by Sofia Kovaleskaya in 1886.
      Kovaleskaya, an accomplished mathematician, novelist and
      feminist, met GE in 1869 and revisited her in 1880. The article is a
      response to Cross's *Life*. A sensitive and intelligent record of her
      meetings with GE and her understanding of the relation of her
      life to her fiction and to society.

19   Haight, Gordon S.
      THE GEORGE ELIOT LETTERS, vols 8 and 9 (New Haven,
      Conn.: Yale University Press, 1978)

      The final two volumes, published almost fifteen years after the
      first seven, include a few new letters by GE, revised versions of
      some letters that appeared earlier, a considerable number of
      letters by G. H. Lewes and by some other of GE's
      correspondents, and a new index.

20   Pratt, John Clark and Neufeldt, Victor A.
      GEORGE ELIOT'S "MIDDLEMARCH" NOTEBOOKS: A
      TRANSCRIPTION (Berkeley: University of California Press,
      1979)

      A record of GE's literary and historical research from 1868 to
      1871. The notebooks are reproduced "as graphically as
      possible", and the notes and references are extensive and
      helpful.

21   Waley, Daniel
      GEORGE ELIOT'S BLOTTER: A COMMONPLACE BOOK
      (London: The British Library, 1980)

      A transcription of GE's reading lists recorded in a British
      Library MS, with brief commentary.

22   Wiesenfarth, Joseph
      A WRITER'S NOTEBOOK, 1854–1879, AND
      UNCOLLECTED WRITINGS (Charlottesville: University of
      Virginia Press, 1981)

      A transcription, with notes and introduction, of GE's longest,
      most comprehensive notebook, which records research for
      Adam Bede and *The Mill on the Floss*, and entries for *The
      Spanish Gypsy, Felix Holt, Romola, Middlemarch* and *Daniel
      Deronda*.

23   Pinion, F. B.
      A GEORGE ELIOT MISCELLANY: A SUPPLEMENT TO
      HER NOVELS (Totowa, N.J.: Barnes and Noble, 1982)

      A pot-pourri of GE's non-novel writing, from her early essays,
      from her journals, poetry and short stories, and from *The
      Confessions of Theophrastus Such*. All had been published
      before.

24   Haight, Gordon S.
      SELECTIONS FROM GEORGE ELIOT'S LETTERS (New
      Haven, Conn.: Yale University Press, 1985)

      An excellent selection from the nine volumes of letters, giving a
      rich sense of GE's life and development. Includes several letters
      hitherto unpublished.

Biographies

25   Cross, J. W.
GEORGE ELIOT'S LIFE AS RELATED IN HER LETTERS
AND JOURNALS, 3 vols (London: Blackwood and Sons, 1885)

Still useful construction of GE's life from her letters and
notebooks: adulatory and to a degree expurgated, yet full of rich
material, including GE's essay on "The Spanish Gypsy and
Tragedy in General".

26   Browning, Oscar
LIFE OF GEORGE ELIOT (London: Walter Scott, 1890)

A personal friend, Browning fills his biography with personal
reminiscences, and connects GE's life with her writings.
Adulatory in its criticism, the book—unusually for its
time—sees GE's novels as becoming increasingly valuable and
profound, so that *Daniel Deronda* is her masterpiece.

27   Deakin, Mary H.
THE EARLY LIFE OF GEORGE ELIOT (Manchester:
Manchester University Press, 1913)

Takes GE's life to 1859, to the point of publication of *Adam
Bede*, on the assumption that "the interest of every person's life
lies" in the years of development. The book has no precise thesis
but intelligently interprets GE's thought and experience,
emphasizing her teaching and wisdom.

28   Cross, Wilbur L.
"George Eliot in Retrospect", *Yale Review*, 9 (1920), 256–70.

Reviews GE's life and reputation, arguing that after *Silas
Marner*, GE lost her perceptive powers "and *Middlemarch* was
the result".

29   Haldane, Elizabeth S.
GEORGE ELIOT AND HER TIMES: A VICTORIAN
STUDY (New York: D. Appleton and Co., 1927)

An early judicious attempt to rectify the excesses of both the early admiration and subsequent depreciation of GE's work. Haldane considers each of the novels critically and biographically, to place them within their historical context.

30   Patterson, Arthur
      GEORGE ELIOT'S FAMILY LIFE AND LETTERS (London: Selwyn and Blount, 1928)

      Letters from Lewes and GE to Lewes's children, and biographical memoir.

31   Freemantle, Anne
      GEORGE ELIOT (London: Duckworth; New York: Macmillan, 1933)

      A study of GE's life in London, drawing on the diaries of John Chapman, in whose house GE first lived when editing the *Westminster Review*. Unsentimental in her approach to GE's attachments to Chapman and Lewes, Freemantle offers a psychological interpretation of GE's preoccupation with moral retribution. Freemantle belongs to that early century tradition of unease with Victorian moral earnestness and celebrates rather the rebellious aspects of GE's life.

32   Kitchel, Anna T.
      GEORGE LEWES AND GEORGE ELIOT (New York: John Day, 1933)

      A useful biography of G.H. Lewes, with considerable information about his life with GE and the interchange between them.

33   Williams, Blanche Colton
      GEORGE ELIOT (New York: Macmillan, 1936)

      Based on acquaintance with surviving relatives and friends of GE, Lewes and Cross.

34   Haight, Gordon S.
      GEORGE ELIOT AND JOHN CHAPMAN. WITH

CHAPMAN'S DIARIES (New Haven, Conn.: Yale University Press, 1940)

Reveals the details of the complicated and difficult relationship between GE and Chapman from their meeting in 1842 through her work on the *Westminster Review*.

35   Speaight, Robert
GEORGE ELIOT (London: Arthur Barker, 1954)

An intelligent introduction to GE, attempting "to find her new friends". A brief and useful biography is followed by a series of chapters on each of the major works. A warm admirer of GE's art, Speaight follows the then recent critical evaluation of GE by F.R. Leavis.

36   McKenzie, K. A.
EDITH SIMCOX AND GEORGE ELIOT (New York and London: Oxford University Press, 1961)

Primarily about the remarkable Edith Simcox, a not very well-known Victorian journalist and thinker, learned, energetic, passionately devoted to GE, who started a shirt factory to employ women, and who won election to the London School Board. McKenzie describes what Gordon Haight calls Simcox's "secret love" of GE. The book suggests much about GE in describing her response to Simcox's advances and idolatry.

37   Haight, Gordon S.
GEORGE ELIOT: A BIOGRAPHY (New York: Oxford University Press, 1968)

The "definitive" biography, based on Haight's great work as editor of the George Eliot Letters, it is carefully conservative and eschews interpretation. Haight clearly takes GE at face value and provides an indispensable factual and detailed account of her life. A marked improvement on Cross's biography, in that it restores much that was omitted and is somewhat less reverential, it nevertheless lacks the engagement and immediacy of the Victorian life-and-letters method Cross used. In its dutiful record of the daily activities of GE, it ensures scholarly credibility at the expense of vital understanding.

38   Laski, Marghanita
        GEORGE ELIOT AND HER WORLD (London: Thames and
        Hudson, 1973)

        A biography, accompanied by photographs and illustrations
        relevant to GE's life and work.

39   Redinger, Ruby
        GEORGE ELIOT: THE EMERGENT SELF (London: Bodley
        Head; Toronto: Random House of Canada, 1975)

        The first important biography after Haight's, this volume is less
        official, more interpretative, and less adulatory than either Cross
        or Haight, but it also provides a more complex sense of GE's
        inner life. Redinger is the first to consider the effect on GE of
        inadequate relations with mother and family. Moreover, she
        considers GE's development in the light of her resistance to
        developing her own narrative talents, and in the light of her
        ultimate achievement in that direction. It does not take the
        detailed accounting of her life past the point at which the writing
        career began. The most important alternative to the more
        "factual" biographies.

40   Nadel, Ira Bruce
        "George Eliot and her Biographers", (Totowa, N.J.: Barnes
        and Noble, 1982), GEORGE ELIOT: A CENTENARY
        TRIBUTE, pp. 107–21 (see 51)

        A very useful survey of the major biographies of GE.

41   Rose, Phyllis
        PARALLEL LIVES: FIVE VICTORIAN MARRIAGES (New
        York: Alfred Knopf, 1983)

        A rereading, novelistically, of the relationship between GE and
        Lewes. A sensitive interpretation of their behaviour, relying on
        letters primarily. Interestingly argues that GE was not the passive
        creation of Lewes, but that she took the initiative. Counters
        Haight's reading by insisting not on GE's need for love, but on
        her desire. A generous and humane reading of GE's life – even
        the marriage to Cross is seen as perfectly understandable and
        good.

42   Williams, David
MR. GEORGE ELIOT: A BIOGRAPHY OF GEORGE
HENRY LEWES (New York: Franklin Watts, 1983)

The tone is consistently and harshly unsympathetic even in its
attempt to aggrandize Lewes at the expense of GE, who reveals in
this study no redeeming social or moral qualities. Lewes is
pictured as a long-suffering self-sacrificing figure who created
GE, "nothing without him", who was important not only in
encouraging but in structuring the writing of the novels. The
book has the virtue of its contentiousness, its attempt to render
the (rather unpleasant) feel of life with parsimonious, unself-
confident, conventionally moral, self-obsessed Marian Evans.
An unrelenting deflation of GE.

Collections of Critical Essays on GE

(With some few exceptions, essays collected in these volumes are not entered separately elsewhere in this bibliography.)

43   Stang, Richard
        DISCUSSIONS OF GEORGE ELIOT (Boston: D. C. Heath, 1960)

        Includes key essays from 1866 to 1959: Henry James, "The Novels of George Eliot"; Henry James, "The Life of George Eliot"; Henry James, "*Daniel Deronda:* A Conversation"; Leslie Stephen, "George Eliot"; Marcel Proust, "Notes on George Eliot"; Virginia Woolf, "George Eliot"; Lord David Cecil, "George Eliot"; S. L. Bethell, "The Novels of George Eliot"; F. R. Leavis, "George Eliot"; V. S. Pritchett, "George Eliot"; Joan Bennett, "Vision and Design"; Basil Willey, "George Eliot"; Barbara Hardy, "Imagery in George Eliot's Last Novels"; Quentin Anderson, "George Eliot in *Middlemarch*"; Jerome Thale, "George Eliot's Fable for Her Times: *Silas Marner*"; Jerome Thale, "The Darkened World: *Daniel Deronda*".

44   Haight, Gordon S.
        A CENTURY OF GEORGE ELIOT CRITICISM (Boston: Houghton Mifflin, 1965)

        Fifty-two essays chronologically arranged from the appearance of *Scenes of Clerical Life* until 1962. An excellent overview of GE's reputation. Materials often sharply abridged.

45   Holmstrom, John and Lerner, Laurence
        GEORGE ELIOT AND HER READERS: A SELECTION OF CONTEMPORARY REVIEWS (New York: Barnes and Noble, 1966)

        The title is self-explanatory. Lerner provides commentary.

46   Creeger, George R.
        GEORGE ELIOT: A COLLECTION OF CRITICAL ESSAYS (Englewood Cliffs, N.J.: Prentice-Hall, 1970)

Collects ten valuable essays, five on individual novels, five on general problems of GE's work: Bernard J. Paris, "George Eliot's Religion of Humanity"; Thomas Pinney, "The Authority of the Past in George Eliot's Novels"; Barbara Hardy, "The Moment of Disenchantment in George Eliot's Novels"; Darrell Mansell, Jr, "George Eliot's Conception of Form"; U. C. Knoepflmacher, "George Eliot, Feuerbach, and the Question of Criticism"; George R. Creeger, "An Interpretation of *Adam Bede*"; George Levine, "Intelligence as Deception: *The Mill on the Floss*"; David R. Carroll, "*Felix Holt*: Society as Protagonist"; Quentin Anderson, "George Eliot in *Middlemarch*"; Henry James, "*Daniel Deronda*: A Conversation".

47   Hardy, Barbara
      CRITICAL ESSAYS ON GEORGE ELIOT (London: Routledge & Kegan Paul, 1970)

      Eight essays specially written for the volume cover each of the novels; two other original essays treat the work more generally: Derek and Sybil Oldfield, "*Scenes of Clerical Life:* The Diagram and the Picture"; John Goode, "*Adam Bede*"; Barbara Hardy, "*The Mill on the Floss*"; Lillian Haddakin, "*Silas Marner*"; George Levine, "*Romola* as Fable"; Arnold Kettle, "*Felix Holt* the Radical"; Isobel Armstrong, "*Middlemarch:* A Note on George Eliot's Wisdom"; Graham Martin, "*Daniel Deronda:* George Eliot and Political Change"; W. J. Harvey, "Idea and Image in the Novels of George Eliot"; John Bayley, "The Pastoral of Intellect".

48   Carroll, David
      GEORGE ELIOT: THE CRITICAL HERITAGE (London: Routledge & Kegan Paul, 1971)

      Carroll collects from five to thirteen reviews of each of the novels, and adds five general overviews of GE's life and career by contemporaries. An indispensable guide to the reception of GE's work.

49   Knoepflmacher, U. C. and Levine, George
      NINETEENTH-CENTURY FICTION SPECIAL ISSUE: GEORGE ELIOT 1880–1980, 35 (1980)

Eight original essays, an original poem by Helen Cooper, and commentary by three distinguished critics, Barbara Hardy, Hillis Miller and Richard Poirier, on a passage from *Middlemarch*. The volume emphasizes the less explored works of GE, including her essays. Margaret Doody, "George Eliot and the Eighteenth Century Novel"; Elaine Showalter, "The Greening of Sister George"; G. Robert Stange, "The Voices of the Essayist"; David Carroll, " 'Janet's Repentance' and the Myth of the Organic"; Joseph Butwin, "The Pacification of the Crowd: From 'Janet's Repentance' to *Felix Holt*"; Catherine Gallagher, "The Failure of Realism: *Felix Holt*"; Martha S. Vogeler, "George Eliot and the Positivists"; K. K. Collins, presents for the first time and with extensive commentary the contents of a GE notebook stamped "Three Essays".

(PRIMARY)

50   Smith, Anne
       GEORGE ELIOT: CENTENARY ESSAYS AND AN
       UNPUBLISHED FRAGMENT (Totowa, N.J.: Barnes and
       Noble, 1980)

Ten original essays, rather disparate in approach and coverage. The new GE MS fragment is described and presented by William Baker. The MS seems to be pages of description from a novel in the planning about 1878. (PRIMARY) Three essays in the volume have to do with *Middlemarch*. Terence Wright, "Critical Approaches to George Eliot"; Graham Martin, "*The Mill on the Floss* and the Unreliable Narrator"; Janet K. Gezari, "*Romola* and the Myth of Apocalypse"; Norman Vance, "Law, Religion and the Unity of *Felix Holt*"; Jan B. Gordon, "Origins, *Middlemarch*, Endings: George Eliot's Crisis of the Antecedent"; George Levine, "The Hero as Dilettante: *Middlemarch* and *Nostromo*"; Susan Meikle, "Fruit and Seed: The Finale to *Middlemarch*"; Bonnie Zimmerman, "Gwendolen Harleth and 'The Girl of the Period' ".

51   Haight, Gordon S. and VanArsdel, Rosemary T.
       GEORGE ELIOT: A CENTENARY TRIBUTE (Totowa, N.J.:
       Barnes and Noble, 1982)

Thirteen very short essays drawn from a centenary conference at Puget Sound. The quality of the essays varies greatly but the brevity precludes important original work. Wiesenfarth's essay on *Romola* is outstanding. Includes: Gordon Haight, "George

Eliot's Bastards''; Juliet McMaster, "George Eliot's Language of the Sense"; Elizabeth A. Daniels, "A Meredithian Glance at Gwendolen Harleth"; Ruth apRoberts, "*Middlemarch* and the New Humanity"; Robert B. Heilman, " 'Stealthy Convergence' in *Middlemarch*"; Joseph Wiesenfarth, "Antique Gems from *Romola* to *Daniel Deronda*"; Martha S. Vogeler, "The Choir Invisible: The Poetics of Humanist Piety"; Jacob Korg, "How George Eliot's People Think"; Miriam H. Berlin, "George Eliot and the Russians"; Ira Bruce Nadel, "George Eliot and her Biographers"; Ian Adam, "The Ambivalence of *The Mill on the Floss*"; Florence Sandler, "The Unity of *Felix Holt*"; John F. Hulcoop, " 'This Petty Medium': In the Middle of *Middlemarch*".

Full-Length Critical Studies

52   Cooke, George Willis
        GEORGE ELIOT: A CRITICAL STUDY (Boston: J. R.
        Osgood; New York: Houghton Mifflin, 1883)

        Although not a biography, this book includes a great deal of
        biographical and social material because, Cooke argues, to
        understand a writer's work one must understand her life and
        milieu. The study of the works is not arranged chronologically
        but thematically. Cooke is unhappy with GE's role as a thinker,
        and finds her agnostic, positivist and scientific ideas inadequate
        and distracting: "Science destroys poetry, dries up the poetic
        sense, closes the doors of imagination"; but he finds her art to be
        rich and imaginative. To evaluate her correctly one must
        separate GE's theories from her artistic genius.

53   Stephen, Leslie
        GEORGE ELIOT (London: Macmillan and Co., 1902)

        A full-scale though concise biography and survey of GE's work.
        Stephen emphasizes her philosophical interests and calls her the
        "first female novelist whose inspiration came in a great degree
        from a philosophical creed." He admires most the two early
        novels and calls the first part of *The Mill on the Floss* "the
        culmination of GE's powers", but sees Stephen Guest as "a mere
        hair-dresser's block". Criticizes the later works for being too
        abstract and depending too much on theory. In *Romola* he
        admires only the title character, who would be impressive if she
        got out of her fifteenth-century costume; *Middlemarch* he finds
        out of touch with reality; *Daniel Deronda* gets perfunctory
        treatment. Stephen is concerned with the relation of ideas to
        fiction, and with the primary importance of personal experience.

54   Bourl'honne, Paul
        ESSAI DE BIOGRAPHIE INTELLECTUELLE ET
        MORALE, 1819–1854 (Paris: Librairie Ancienne Honoré
        Champion, 1933; repr. New York: AMS Press, 1973)

        An early but very useful accounting of GE's intellectual
        background, with particular emphasis on Feuerbach, Comte
        and Spinoza, and the whole positivist/humanist tradition.
                                                    (PHILOSOPHY)

55   Bullett, Gerald
       GEORGE ELIOT: HER LIFE AND BOOKS (London: Collins;
       New Haven, Conn.: Yale University Press, 1947)

       An interesting but ultimately characteristic condescending
       treatment of GE, reflecting earlier Bloomsbury revulsion of her
       moralism and grudgingly allowing that she sometimes succeeds
       in spite of herself.

56   Bennett, Joan
       GEORGE ELIOT: HER MIND AND HER ART (Cambridge:
       Cambridge University Press, 1948)

       The first three chapters of this volume are biographical. The last
       eight examine the novels in detail. Bennett argues that GE was
       the greatest novelist of her time and that her work pointed
       forward to later developments in the novel. Sometimes, the
       interest in exploration of character (like Maggie's, for example)
       is incompatible with the spacious and panoramic qualities of
       GE's work, which is equally interested in social context.

57   Cooper, Lettice
       GEORGE ELIOT: WRITERS AND THEIR WORKS
       (London: published for the British Council by Longmans,
       Green, 1951)

       A very brief introductory survey of GE's life and work, with
       short bibliography.

58   Hardy, Barbara
       THE NOVELS OF GEORGE ELIOT: A STUDY IN FORM
       (London: Athlone Press; New York: Oxford University Press,
       1959)

       This was the most influential early full-scale critical study of
       George Eliot's art in the revival of critical interest in her work at
       mid-century. The book remains one of the very best in its minute
       and careful analysis of the formal and thematic elements of GE's
       art. Hardy demonstrates GE's structural power and critical
       intelligence as she analyses narrative patterns, character types,
       recurrent images, authorial voice, formal techniques, and the
       interrelation among all as she proves that "George Eliot's
       composition is usually as complex as the composition of Henry
       James or Proust or Joyce."

59   Stump, Reva
        MOVEMENT AND VISION IN GEORGE ELIOT'S NOVELS
        (Seattle: University of Washington Press, 1959)

An interesting set of very detailed readings of three novels: *Adam Bede, The Mill on the Floss* and *Middlemarch*. Stump detects a fundamental pattern of movement towards vision in all of the novels, and subtly and intelligently sustains a sense of the uniqueness of each book. This volume made a valuable contribution to the developing study of GE's special formal achievements in the novels.

60   Thale, Jerome
        THE NOVELS OF GEORGE ELIOT (New York: Columbia
        University Press, 1959)

Another important contribution to the revival of interest in George Eliot. Thale analyses each of the novels, emphasizing GE's learning and intelligence as they combined with her understanding and concern for domestic detail.

61   Harvey, W. J.
        THE ART OF GEORGE ELIOT (New York: Oxford University
        Press, 1962)

One of the major documents in the revival of critical interest in George Eliot, the volume consolidates important individual essays written earlier, in particular, "The Omniscient Author Convention" of 1957 revised as chapter 3. Harvey analyses and validates George Eliot's formal achievements as novelist in the context of a time when formal, Jamesian criteria were dominant. Harvey was right to say that "We stand . . . on the brink of a great leap forward in our understanding and appreciation of Victorian fiction"; and in his bringing together formal analysis with an understanding of George Eliot's moral preoccupations, his book was an important preliminary step to the leap that followed.

62   Allen, Walter
        GEORGE ELIOT (New York: Macmillan; London: Weidenfeld
        and Nicolson, 1964)

Half-biography, half-critical study, this is very much an

introduction and unfortunately perpetuates through emphasis the distorted and often irrelevant view that GE had no sympathy with pretty women. Very much a traditional, pre-feminist, male perspective.

63   Paris, Bernard J.
        EXPERIMENTS IN LIFE: GEORGE ELIOT'S QUEST FOR VALUES (Detroit: Wayne State University Press, 1965)

The first full-length study in English of George Eliot's intellectual development. Paris explores intellectual influences and George Eliot's ideas on human values and human nature, touching on epistemological, anthropological and aesthetic questions. He traces the basic pattern of moral development in GE's work and studies most of the novels from these perspectives, finding in her own work the same three stages of development she finds in her protagonists.

                                                        (PHILOSOPHY)

64   Knoepflmacher, U. C.
        GEORGE ELIOT'S EARLY NOVELS: THE LIMITS OF REALISM (Berkeley: University of California Press, 1968)

The most important study of the development of George Eliot's art through mid-career. Knoepflmacher takes the reader through the stages of her intellectual growth and reads each novel in the light of the previous one, showing how GE takes up problems inadequately resolved and experiments again in a new way. GE's commitment to realism is in practice deeply modified in her presentation of characters not at all ordinary, like "Amos Barton", but idealized, like Adam Bede.

65   Milner, Ian
        THE STRUCTURE OF VALUES IN GEORGE ELIOT'S NOVELS (Praha: Universita Karlova. Acta Universitätis Carolinae Philogica Monographia 23, 1968)

Emphasizes the way in which history, and the social, moral and intellectual context, impinge on the characters and on the working-out of the novels.

66   Auster, Henry

LOCAL HABITATIONS: REGIONALISM IN THE EARLY
NOVELS OF GEORGE ELIOT (Cambridge, Mass.: Harvard
University Press, 1970)

Regionalism for Auster is concern with a locale in the interests of
the larger aims of art, and he locates this as an initiating source
for GE's novels. The readings of the novels that follow the initial
chapters on "regionalism" do not develop the idea very much
although they are much concerned with "background". The
question of the importance of regionalism to GE's art remains
open.

67   Bonaparte, Felicia
     WILL AND DESTINY: MORALITY AND TRAGEDY IN
     GEORGE ELIOT'S NOVELS (New York: New York
     University Press, 1975)

Singles out GE's tragic vision as the most important aspect of her
work, which speaks directly to our contemporary condition.
Explores GE's idea of the tragic, her self-conscious attempt to
make her novels tragic and to revise tragedy for her own time.
The Greek tragic confrontation with the gods is replaced in GE's
imagination with the confrontation between human will and
natural destiny. Retribution is inevitable, as in Greek drama, and
out of the conflict arises human morality, requiring choices and
sympathy in a world incompatible with human desire. The book
does not proceed novel by novel but explores its categories —
will, destiny, morality, knowledge — in relation to their place in
GE's aesthetic working-out of the problems.

68   Roberts, Neil
     GEORGE ELIOT: HER BELIEFS AND HER ART (London:
     Elek Books; Pittsburgh: University of Pittsburgh Press, 1975)

An attempt to "examine GE's moral, social and religious ideas
as elements in her artistic creation." Assumes that GE knows
little of the consequences of the social and industrial revolution
around her but is uniquely qualified to read the private moral
and psychological life of her characters. Sees her as honest
confronter of moral truths, and takes the task of criticism to test
his sense of life against that of the writer. After a general
summary of her moral and intellectual positions, with emphasis
on Comte and Feuerbach, proceeds to critical analysis of each
novel. Very much in the mode of F. R. Leavis, without his
originality or acuteness.

69   Emery, Laura Comer
        GEORGE ELIOT'S CREATIVE CONFLICT: THE OTHER
        SIDE OF SILENCE (Berkeley: University of California Press,
        1976)

        A fairly strict Freudian interpretation of the novels. Self-denial is
        perceived as neurotic repression of Oedipal hostilities and fear of
        genital maturity. The novels disguise a "latent" content, and the
        real movement is through self-confrontation that exposes the
        oedipal crisis, that leads to death at the end of *The Mill on the
        Floss* and to a new maturity in Dorothea's unrepressed choice of
        Ladislaw as sexual mate. Through the novels, GE creatively
        restructures her defences.

70   Liddell, Robert
        THE NOVELS OF GEORGE ELIOT (London: Duckworth;
        New York: St Martin's Press, 1977)

        An old-fashioned introduction to the novels, limited by its
        simplifications of critical issues, its excess of plot summary, and
        its failure to refer to any GE scholarship.

71   Wiesenfarth, Joseph
        GEORGE ELIOT'S MYTHMAKING (Heidelberg: Carl
        Winter, 1977)

        Examines in detail the significant mythical allusions and patterns
        GE used in her novels to create her own "stories of creation,
        destruction, redemption, and a search for a paradise in the
        context of a secularized nineteenth-century view of man".
        Careful analyses of each novel and of the development of GE's
        use of mythical pattern.

72   Mintz, Alan
        GEORGE ELIOT AND THE NOVEL OF VOCATION
        (Cambridge, Mass.: Harvard University Press, 1978)

        The true Victorian *Bildungsroman* is the novel of vocation, and
        vocation itself supplants romance as the major subject. The
        question of vocation, moreover, is allied to the woman question,
        for Victorian women like Dorothea and Rosamond must ask,
        "What can I do?" Mintz shows that the ideal of vocation carries
        with it a religious tradition that leads easily to self-

aggrandizement and hypocrisy in a secular society. A rich exploration of the way a major cultural change affected GE's art.

73   Fisher, Philip
MAKING UP SOCIETY: THE NOVELS OF GEORGE ELIOT (Pittsburgh: University of Pittsburgh Press, 1981)

Primarily concerned to trace GE's treatment of the self, conceived always in relation to society. Fisher defines a movement through the novels, culminating in *Middlemarch*, from a sense of society there to be discovered, to a sense of society as a kind of creation. A counter-strain is the heroic novel, which tends to idealize a central figure, and where GE's special genius for seeing truth as tentative, engaged and generous, is displaced by a sense of a truth — an idea — there to be discovered. Unfortunately, the book lacks almost any reference to a community of scholarship, and the *Daniel Deronda* section is hurt particularly because it does not recognize its own conventionality or the fascinating recent work which has revised our sense of GE.

74   Newton, K. M.
GEORGE ELIOT: ROMANTIC HUMANIST (Totowa, N.J.: Barnes and Noble, 1981)

Treats GE as a philosophical novelist, and attempts to shift emphasis from her positivism to her place in the Romantic tradition. Despite a rhetoric that implies the originality of his arguments, Newton essentially recapitulates her views and her relation of Lewes's ideas. GE replaces God and intellect with feeling, with inheritance, with community (which shares feelings and controls them). Feeling is given super-personal control by community, formerly the Church. Morality is a language of feeling. Dealing with the potentially disruptive element of "impulse" thus becomes a major GE theme.

75   Hardy, Barbara
PARTICULARITIES: READINGS IN GEORGE ELIOT (Athens: Ohio University Press; London: Peter Owen, 1982)

An interesting collection of essays from perhaps the best critic of GE, ranging from an outstanding essay on *Middlemarch* from

The Appropriate Form to recent essays, somewhat less impressive, on general themes and characteristics of the novels. All the essays are marked by remarkable precision of perception and detail.

76   Putzell-Korab, Sara M.
THE EVOLVING CONSCIOUSNESS: AN HEGELIAN READING OF THE NOVELS OF GEORGE ELIOT (Salzburg: Institut für Anglistik and Amerikanistik, 1982)

Putzell argues the significance and applicability of Hegel to George Eliot's fiction. She rejects the traditional dualistic reading of GE — the split between sympathy and egoism — for a more dialectical reading, where each becomes a condition of the other. "Although all of [GE's] protagonists can be said to learn sympathy, comparison with Hegel's phenomenology of individual development makes it possible to describe differences among their structurally similar histories."

(PHILOSOPHY)

77   Ashton, Rosemary
GEORGE ELIOT (New York: Oxford University Press, 1983)

A very general and perfunctory introduction.

78   Mann, Karen B.
THE LANGUAGE THAT MAKES GEORGE ELIOT'S FICTION (Baltimore: Johns Hopkins University Press, 1983)

Argues that GE saw in her language the best means to register her sense of the world, to grasp that world. Mann tries to get at the dual nature of GE's language — which aspires to reference to the world and to itself. Most of the book is devoted to basic metaphors, as they connect with basic strategies of all her fiction.

79   Graver, Suzanne
GEORGE ELIOT AND COMMUNITY: A STUDY IN SOCIAL THEORY AND FICTIONAL FORM (Berkeley: University of California Press, 1984)

A reading of GE's fiction in the context of pre- and unMarxist traditions of social theory. Graver argues that the theoretical underpinning of GE's fiction was the attempt to create a community of readers to prepare the evolution of a new *Gemeinschaft* that would mix modernity with tradition and unify thought and action. The unresolvable tension between theory and fact, multiplicity and particularity, the abstract and the concrete, is part of the creative openness of GE's art. GE's art is both a formulation of her programme and, in its insistence on the particular individual, subversive of theory.

80   Myers, William
THE TEACHINGS OF GEORGE ELIOT (Leicester: Leicester University Press; Totowa, N.J.: Barnes and Noble, 1984)

An ostensibly old-fashioned description of GE's ideas and sources, this is a major contribution to our understanding and evaluation of her work. Myers attempts to determine what GE intended, taking seriously her didacticism, arguing that disregard of intention in modern criticism is both intrinsically falsifying and particularly inapplicable to GE. The first part explicates her beliefs — humanist, positivist, scientific, determinist, aesthetic. The second part subjects these views to radical critiques, using Marx, Freud, Lacan and Nietzsche as formulators of positions that not only negate GE's views, but her didactic strategy of privileged, contemplative, materialist teaching. The final section, "Affirmations", shows GE's own anticipations of or response to the criticisms levelled in the second part.

(PHILOSOPHY)

81   Ermarth, Elizabeth Deeds
GEORGE ELIOT (Boston: Twayne Publishers, 1985)

Part of the Twayne series, this is a brief introduction to GE, but conducted at a higher level than most such introductions. Ermarth has a firm and original perspective on GE and argues that the volume attempts to "formulate a vocabulary that acknowledges the coherence of form and control and does justice to the complexity and elegance of her work."

82   Welsh, Alexander
GEORGE ELIOT AND BLACKMAIL (Cambridge, Mass.: Harvard University Press, 1986)

A brilliant analysis of GE and her work from the perspective of the information explosion of the nineteenth century. Welsh shows how as information itself came to have monetary value, the tendency to steal and compete for it increased. He links this development to important social changes that manifest themselves in GE's novels, with their emphasis on characters with hidden pasts, and finally links this pattern to Freudian analysis, which he shows to have been anticipated by GE's narratives.

General Essays on George Eliot

(See also Wright in 50; Harvey and Bayley in 47)

83   James, Henry
"The Novels of George Eliot", *Atlantic Monthly*, 18 (1866), 479–92

An overview, in the midst of GE's career, of her work to that point. Her strengths are in portraits of "common people", and her novels focus on the contest between passion and conscience. Finds weakness in titular heroes and her strength in description rather than drama. "The author is, in morals and aesthetics, essentially a conservative."

84   Dowden, Edward
"George Eliot", "Middlemarch and Daniel Deronda" and "The Scientific Movement in Literature", STUDIES IN LITERATURE, 1789–1877 (London: Kegan Paul, 1879), pp. 85–121; 240–310

"George Eliot" interestingly formulates the idea of the writer's "second self", who writes the books and lives and speaks through them. The most vivid thing about GE's work is this second self, who is a great nature, has suffered, and whose struggle towards truth will be triumphant. The self is compassionate, undogmatic, fusing the moral and artistic. Conscience is at the centre of her work. Dowden's unqualified praise might usefully be compared with James's more measured admiration. "Middlemarch and Daniel Deronda" argues for the breadth and height of GE's genius, seeing the two novels as companion pieces, one prosaic and critical, the other poetical and constructive. The essay on science is a major Victorian statement about the moral and religious implications of the new science, which Dowden celebrates as a great inspiration for art.

85   Ruskin, John
"Fiction — Fair and Foul", *Nineteenth Century*, 7 (1880), 941–63; 10 (1881), 515–31

In this remarkable tirade against "modern" fiction, which is held up against the model of Scott and which Ruskin takes to reflect the disease of the new urban culture, George Eliot (particularly in *The Mill on the Floss*) is dismissed as trivial and inordinately preoccupied with banal people in banal situations. "The leavings of the Pentonville trolley", describes GE's work; and her characters are victims of "cutaneous disease".

86   Simcox, Edith
       "George Eliot", *Nineteenth Century*, 9 (1881), 778–801

       An admiring survey of the life and works, written by GE's friend (see 36). Simcox emphasizes the sympathy and moral greatness of GE, in her life and in her art.

87   Myers, F. W. H.
       "George Eliot", ESSAYS — MODERN (London: Macmillan, 1885), 251–75

       The famous melancholy essay in which Myers writes, shortly after GE's death, of his "deeply venerated" friend. Myers' biographical sketch gives us in essence the solemn and intellectually powerful Victorian sage. Myers' own spiritualist concern with the possibility of an afterlife made GE's stoic materialism fascinating to him. Here he describes her commitment to the idea of God, Immortality, Duty, and her pronouncement: "how inconceivable was the first, how unbelievable the second, and yet how peremptory and absolute the third."   (BIOGRAPHY)

88   Hutton, R. H.
       "George Eliot as Author", "George Eliot's Life and Letters", ESSAYS ON SOME OF THE MODERN GUIDES OF ENGLISH THOUGHT IN MATTERS OF FAITH (London: Macmillan and Co., 1887), pp. 145–300

       Admiring and intelligent studies of GE, emphasizing her secular morality, analysing the narrative treatment of characters' struggles with conscience and resistance to the past — punished always by Nemesis. Hutton finds her artistic weakness to be in her scepticism.

89   Harrison, Frederic
       "George Eliot", STUDIES IN EARLY VICTORIAN LITERATURE (London: Edward Arnold, 1895; repr. 1901), pp. 205–24

A slight essay but interesting because Harrison, who knew George Eliot well and wrote about her often, looks back here after the sinking of her reputation to consider her real strengths. He emphasizes weaknesses but still looks at her admiringly.

90   Brunetière, Ferdinand
"English Naturalism: a Study of George Eliot", LE ROMAN NATURALISTE (Paris: Calmann-Lévy, 1896), pp. 205–52

An important statement about naturalism. Brunetière compares French (Roman Catholic) to English (Protestant) naturalism, and finds the French wanting in sympathy, which, he says, is the soul of naturalism. Sympathy is the condition for GE's profound psychology, metaphysical solidity and great morality, whereas art for art sake is peculiarly "Latin". Admires in particular *Adam Bede* and *The Mill on the Floss* and finds in them a triumph of psychological description. Nevertheless, GE is unequal to the brilliance of construction and art to be found in Flaubert and Balzac, and he concludes by asking whether it is possible to bring together great art with sympathy.

91   Linton, Eliza Lynn
MY LITERARY LIFE (London: Hodder & Stoughton, 1899)

Includes Linton's notorious attack on GE.

92   Oliphant, James
VICTORIAN NOVELISTS (London: Blackie and Sons, 1899; New York: Harper and Brothers, 1901), 78–148

An early critical appraisal that places GE in the first rank of novelists and defends her power of narration, her use of authorial commentary and her "moral pedantry".

93   Woolf, Virginia
"George Eliot", THE COMMON READER (New York: Harcourt, Brace, and World, 1925), pp. 166–76

A remarkable appreciation of GE, noting that *Middlemarch* is one of the few English novels written for grown-ups.

94   Parlett, Mathilde M.

"The Influence of Contemporary Criticism on George Eliot", *Studies in Philology*, 30 (1933), 103–32

Argues that GE's reputation improves as critics recognize the superiority of the later novels (from *Romola* on) to the earlier ones. Despite GE's attempt to avoid contemporary criticism, she was affected by it, and the shift to the later style is partly a response to the criticism.

95   Cecil, Lord David
     EARLY VICTORIAN NOVELISTS: ESSAYS IN REVALUATION (London: Constable, 1934), pp. 309–36

An early effort to repair the reputation of Victorian fiction. Cecil identifies GE as "the first modern novelist", an innovator concerned with theological and philosophical issues and possessed with a great command of form.

96   Baker, Ernest A.
     THE HISTORY OF THE ENGLISH NOVEL; vol. 8, FROM THE BRONTËS TO MEREDITH: ROMANTICISM IN THE ENGLISH NOVEL (London: N.F. and G. Witherby, 1937), 221–73

Surveys each of GE's novels and credits her with introducing a philosophy and a new note of seriousness into the English novel.

97   Pritchett, V. S.
     THE LIVING NOVEL (London: Chatto and Windus, 1946; New York: Reynal and Hitchcock, 1947)

An informal but insightful meditation on GE's will, her sympathy and her moral judgement.

98   Hough, Graham
     "Novelist — Philosophers — XII — George Eliot", *Horizon*, 17 (1948), 50–62

One of the best of the pre-Leavis essays on George Eliot; this takes GE's powers of reflection seriously and connects her intelligence and moral seriousness with the quality of her art.

99   Schorer, Mark
"Fiction and the Matrix of Analogy", *Kenyon Review*, 11 (1949), 539–60

One of the most influential critical essays of the period, it takes *Middlemarch* as one of several exemplary novels, showing how metaphor and analogy help shape the structure and significances of narrative.

(MIDDLEMARCH)

100   Bissell, Claude T.
"Social Analysis in the Novels of George Eliot", *English Literary History*, 8 (1951), 221–39

Bissell discusses the novels by focusing on GE's treatment of character within the context of society, arguing that the private self and society can never be regarded apart from each other.

101   Holloway, John
THE VICTORIAN SAGE: STUDIES IN ARGUMENT (New York: St Martin's Press, 1953; Hamden, Conn.: Archon Books, 1962; New York: W. W. Norton, 1965), pp. 11–57

Includes an extensive chapter on GE, placing her as one of the Victorian sages, both on the grounds of her major intellectual concerns and of her formal and rhetorical strategies. As he does with the other "sages", Holloway intelligently describes and analyses GE's overall view of life and morals, and shows how GE's arguments depend not so much on their intellectual coherence as on her capacity to make them felt experientially, through devices of rhetoric or narrative technique.

102   Leavis, F. R.
THE GREAT TRADITION: GEORGE ELIOT, HENRY JAMES, AND JOSEPH CONRAD (London: George W. Stewart, 1948; New York: Doubleday, 1954), pp. 28–125

Perhaps the most influential (if controversial) essay in the revival of interest in George Eliot. Leavis reads GE as a serious moralist, a profound thinker and great psychologist. He carves up the canon into the weak and strong, finding GE susceptible to sentimental lapses of self-indulgence, as at the end of *The Mill on the Floss*, in the treatment of Dorothea in the last half of

Middlemarch, and in the Deronda half of *Daniel Deronda*. His evaluations, including his celebration of the portrait of Mrs Transome in *Felix Holt*, withstood at least thirty years of analysis and criticism.

103   Proust, Marcel
"Notes on George Eliot", CONTRE SAINT-BEUVE (1954), repr. MARCEL PROUST ON ART AND LITERATURE (London: Chatto and Windus, 1957; Meridian Books, 1958)

Interesting commentary of the great novelist on *Adam Bede*. Emphasizes GE's sensitive portrayal of the humble.

104   Kaminsky, Alice R.
"George Eliot, George Henry Lewes, and the Novel", *PMLA*, 70 (1955), 997–1013

Discusses Lewes's theory of naturalism in relation to George Eliot's ideas and her subsequent practice. Lewes's theories of the novel emphasize the moral value of art, the seriousness of fiction and the importance of "modified realism, of psychological characterization, and of formal unity". They were a primary influence on GE's theory of the novel, with its "inimitable blend of psychological realism and philosophic substance".

105   Praz, Mario
THE HERO IN ECLIPSE IN VICTORIAN FICTION, trans. Angus Davidson (London: Oxford University Press, 1956), pp. 319–83

Treating the literature as in the tradition of "Biedermeier", a middle-class tradition focusing not on the remarkable but on the qualities of middle-class life, Praz reads GE as a Wordsworthian writer seeking sympathy for ordinary people in ordinary circumstances.

106   Hyde, William J.
"George Eliot and the Climate of Realism", *PMLA*, 72 (1957), 147–64

Working from GE's "Natural History of German Life", Hyde describes GE's sense of the unpleasant coarseness of the peasant. For the most part, GE does *not* treat such characters centrally.

Her "peasants" are treated very differently from Hardy's, who often are central and capable of more than animal feeling and morality. GE's realism is controlled by her own moral positions.

107   Carroll, David R.
"An Image of Disenchantment in the Novels of George Eliot", *Review of English Studies*, 11 (1960), 29–41.

Suggests the basic pattern of all GE's novels, the movement from illusion into self-knowledge through disenchantment. Subtly indicates major images GE uses to produce this crisis and new self-knowledge.

108   Allott, Miriam
"George Eliot in the 1860's", *Victorian Studies*, 5 (1961), 93–108

The decade was often a period of illness and depression for GE, and the personal difficulties were compounded by growing scepticism and the related "ebbing" of creative vitality. Allott describes GE's writing of the 1860s as evidence of "a period of painful readjustment and recuperation", necessary for revitalization of her imagination. Tragedy and the tragic collision allowed her to work through to the great achievement of *Middlemarch*.

109   Cox, C. B.
"George Eliot: The Conservative Reformer", THE FREE SPIRIT: A STUDY OF LIBERAL HUMANISM IN THE NOVELS OF GEORGE ELIOT, HENRY JAMES, E. M. FORSTER, VIRGINIA WOOLF, ANGUS WILSON (London: Oxford University Press, 1963), pp. 13–37

GE recognizes the drawbacks of liberal individualism and seeks for compensation and fulfilment in regarding the individual within the context of larger social structures. Finds her moral positions simplistic.

110   Feltes, N. N.
"George Eliot and the Unified Sensibility", *PMLA*, 79 (1964), 130–36

Middlemarch and GE's other works reveal her struggle towards a unification of sensibility and "express a view of the human personality in which *wholeness* is all, a view remarkably close to that expressed by G. H. Lewes in *Problems of Life and Mind*."

111   Adam, Ian
        "Character and Destiny in George Eliot's Fiction", *Nineteenth-Century Fiction*, 20 (1965), 127–43

Considers how GE deals with a "deanthropomorphized" world. Through her characters, GE demonstrates her belief in human freedom. *Adam Bede* focuses on characters whose fates seem to be determined by heredity and egoism. The hero describes the basic pattern of GE's novels, from egoism through disenchantment to self-knowledge, and emphasizes the anti-deterministic implications of the characters' movement to choice.

112   Knoepflmacher, U. C.
        RELIGIOUS HUMANISM AND THE VICTORIAN NOVEL: GEORGE ELIOT, WALTER PATER, AND SAMUEL BUTLER (Princeton: Princeton University Press, 1965), pp. 24–148

Attempts to read GE by seeing the intellectual and formal elements of her art as conjoined, not separate. GE "successfully transmuted ideas into form in her novels". In order to show this Knoepflmacher begins by rehearsing three aspects of her thought which he regards as essential to her novels: "her scientific positivism, her 'humanization' of Christianity, and her Arnold-like belief in the force of tradition".

113   Pinney, Thomas
        "The Authority of the Past in George Eliot's Novels", *Nineteenth-Century Fiction*, 21 (1966), 131–47

Locates the core of all of GE's novels in strength and piety of feeling. Affection is understood through the development of early and deep attachment to places, and GE agrees with Wordsworth that "the experiences of childhood are the root of piety." Pinney traces these motifs through the novels, finding in *The Spanish Gypsy* another development, also Wordsworthian, though like that experienced in his later years: authority no longer resides in the past but rather in inherited duty and hereditary claims of race.

114   Lerner, Laurence
THE TRUTHTELLERS: JANE AUSTEN, GEORGE ELIOT, D. H. LAWRENCE (London: Chatto and Windus; New York: Schocken Books, 1967), pp. 235–78

Regards GE as "the finest of all English novelists". Lerner "aims to discover and compare the values of these three writers", with the emphasis on moral rather than aesthetic issues. Looks at GE's secular analogues to religious attitudes and actions and traces a pattern of "hardness, suffering, and awakening" in several novels, the great achievement of the characters being their capacity to feel for and with others. GE combined the best aspects of Austen and Lawrence, "appreciating the value of impulse and surrender". In *The Mill on the Floss* we have a unique instance in GE of impulse replacing morality.

115   Mansell Jr, Darrell
"George Eliot's Conception of Tragedy", *Nineteenth-Century Fiction*, 22 (1967), 155–71

Considers how GE applies Aristotle's *Poetics* to her fiction. Charles Bray's *The Philosophy of Necessity*, with its emphasis on "invariability of sequence", was also important to GE. Ultimately, "her heroic characters are not fit for a world governed by the inexorable law of consequences", but their failures are more admirable than others' prudent calculation of results.

116   Miller, J. Hillis
THE FORM OF VICTORIAN FICTION: THACKERAY, DICKENS, TROLLOPE, GEORGE ELIOT, MEREDITH, AND HARDY (South Bend, Indiana: University of Notre Dame Press, 1968)

Miller sees the secularization of Victorian culture and consciousness leading to a novel of intersubjectivity. He takes GE as the clearest instance of a writer who rejects transcendental authority for social authority, and who sees society as generating itself. Her narrative stance is to take up the position not of a god but of a community capable of entering the consciousness of its individual members.

117   Williams, Raymond
THE ENGLISH NOVEL FROM DICKENS TO LAWRENCE (London: Chatto and Windus; New York: Oxford University Press, 1970), pp. 75–94

Williams says that the novel as a modern form begins with a sense of the compatibility of the social and the individual and increasingly finds that the satisfaction of both is impossible. GE's particular genius lies in drawing the restrictions and limitations of society and of consciousness. Williams sees in GE the Romantic "commitment to a personal vision and a passionate concern with the social experiences of ordinary life". GE's technique isolates her from her own characters and emphasizes the individual experience over the communal.

118   Kroeber, Karl
STYLES IN FICTIONAL STRUCTURE: THE ART OF JANE AUSTEN, CHARLOTTE BRONTË, GEORGE ELIOT (Princeton: Princeton University Press, 1971)

Although Kroeber here attempts a computer analysis of styles, in the long run the book is most useful as a rather unscientific, intuitional analysis of the way the styles work. Clearly, in the course of the study, Kroeber came to understand this.

119   Myers, William
"George Eliot: Politics and Personality", LITERATURE AND POLITICS IN THE NINETEENTH CENTURY, ed. John Lucas (London: Methuen, 1971)

GE's distrust of politics does not extend to "theoretic belief". GE is more concerned with the moral struggle that underlies practical politics than with the politics themselves: "personality is the central political fact in both Positivist theory and GE's novels". For GE historical realities are forced from visions and theories. This position allows her to question her own positions in ways other novelists – like Trollope and Dickens – could not. Usually very precise in her thinking on history and politics, she becomes vague at times because she sees real causes as behind history, not in the events themselves. GE nevertheless faces the "overwhelming human importance of history and . . . its indifference to the individual".

120   Bedient, Calvin
       ARCHITECTS OF THE SELF: GEORGE ELIOT, D. H. LAWRENCE AND E. M. FORSTER (Berkeley: University of California Press, 1972)

       Attacks GE for her repudiation of impulse and of all anti-social actions. The moral model should be Lawrence rather than GE.

121   Williams, Raymond
       THE COUNTRY AND THE CITY (New York: Oxford University Press, 1973), pp. 166–81

       The traditional novel of country and provincial life depends upon a knowable community. Although GE restores rural inhabitants to the novel, they are knowable only in "a deeply inauthentic" though socially successful way. The later novels, except *Middlemarch*, are marked by disturbance and unease resulting from the relationships between individual and community. GE's failure to come to terms with any contemporary society is connected to her attempt to focus on the individual sensibility and to place communal value in the past.

122   Ermarth, Elizabeth
       "Incarnations: George Eliot's Conception of 'Undeviating Law' ", *Nineteenth- Century Fiction*, 29 (1974), 273–86

       Attempts to work out the paradox in GE's conception of "undeviating law" and moral consequences, and her belief in the power of choice and the possibility of alternatives. Ermarth argues that the model for moral law in GE is not scientific or "natural", but cultural. And cultural law "is never impersonal but always 'warmly incarnate', determinate but not deterministic". The essay considers the difference between "cultural" and "natural" law as explored in GE's non-fiction and in her novels.

123   Miller, J. Hillis
       "Narrative and History", *ELH*, 41 (1974), 455–73

This is one of the most important essays in deconstructive rereading of nineteenth-century fiction. Fiction and history share the same assumptions of teleology, causality, unity, progress, linearity, Providence and representation. Miller argues that in *Middlemarch*, GE sees history as "an act of repetition in which the present takes possession of the past and liberates it for a present purpose, thereby exploding the continuum of history." Miller's reading is self-consciously against the grain of traditional understandings of GE's commitment to gradualist history. He argues that the novel subverts the system of history by presenting a view of artistic form as "inorganic, acentered, discontinuous". Miller insistently exposes inconsistencies in GE's rhetoric and narrative structures, and challenges the view that her novels espouse a vision of a "binding theory" that will connect all things.

(MIDDLEMARCH)

124   Auster, Henry
"George Eliot and the Modern Temper", THE WORLDS OF VICTORIAN FICTION, Harvard English Studies, 6, ed. J. H. Buckley (Cambridge, Mass. and London: Harvard University Press, 1975), pp. 75–101

Notes the way the late novels were met with puzzlement and disappointment, like modernist work – but not quite. Examines various modernist aspects of the late novels. Auster notes their scientific concerns, their interiority, but shows that the argument for their modernity is inappropriate. What is missing is "the idea of apocalypse and its consequences for the imagination". What remains of her claims to modernity are, Auster argues, "unity of being and creative imagination". Auster defines these ideas (showing the Romantic roots and their modern manifestations) and discusses several GE novels as examples.

125   Benson, James D.
" 'Sympathetic' Criticism: George Eliot's Response to Contemporary Reviewing", *Nineteenth-Century Fiction*, 29 (1975), 428–40

GE surely knew how her work was being received despite Lewes's attempts to keep reviews from her. She objected to piecemeal criticism and admired "sympathetic" criticism, which regarded novels as wholes and attempted to understand the relations among their themes, characters, parts. GE's views on criticism were ultimately ambivalent: "For all her willingness to discuss form in art . . . she seems equally willing to subordinate artistic unity to the naked confrontation of the reader with insight."

126   Marcus, Steven
        "Human Nature, Social Order, and Nineteenth-Century Systems of Explanation: Starting in with George Eliot", *Salmagundi*, 28 (1975), 20–42

Raises two questions that have much exercised GE criticism: (1) Given GE's exposure of the limits of perspective for all of her characters, how can she give her narrative voice omniscience and authority? (2) How is it possible, given the fact of circumcision, that Daniel Deronda did not know he was Jewish?

127   Beaty, Jerome
        "On First Looking Into George Eliot's *Middlemarch*", THE VICTORIAN EXPERIENCE: THE NOVELISTS, ed. Richard Levine (Athens, Ohio: Ohio University Press, 1976), pp. 151–76

A personal essay on how the author became involved in the study of George Eliot. Beaty describes the early critical battles about the two GEs, woman/man; feeling/intellect. He then discusses his first view of a GE MS, of *Daniel Deronda*, in his early attempt to show that both parts of the novel were equally self-conscious; this enterprise led him to the MS of *Middlemarch* and his ultimate project, listed in 310. But Beaty interestingly traces GE's road to that novel through her inclination in the 1860s to abandon fiction for poetry. Beaty very nicely analyses the ways GE read her personal narratives into the texture of history, and talks of her "stereoscopic" vision, which he finds still illuminating in our own time.

128   Christ, Carol
        "Aggression and Providential Death in George Eliot's Fiction", *Novel*, 9 (1976), 130–40

The many providential deaths in GE's novels, which usually end troubled relationships and satisfy the survivors' need for aggression, enable GE to avoid and prohibit aggression and reveal her reluctance "to abandon the idea of benevolent providence".

129   Eagleton, Terry
        CRITICISM AND IDEOLOGY (London: Verso Editions,
        1978), pp. 110–25

        GE's work attempts "to resolve a structural conflict" between
        Romantic individualism and "certain 'higher' corporate
        ideological modes". Comtism seems to provide a means to
        affirm Romantic values while resisting the dangers of unbridled
        individualism. In practice, however, GE sets up potentially
        tragic collisions "between 'corporate' and 'individualist'
        ideologies" and represses them in the form of the novels.
        Analysis of the novels shows them to be attempts to "integrate
        liberal ideology . . . with certain pre-industrial, idealist or
        positivist organic models".

130   Lerner, Lawrence
        "Literature and Social Change", *Journal of English Studies*, 7
        (1977), 231–52

        Discusses nineteenth-century conceptions of a mobile society by
        examining a number of nineteenth-century novels. *Middlemarch*
        is discussed in passing.

131   King, Jeannette
        TRAGEDY IN THE VICTORIAN NOVEL: THEORY AND
        PRACTICE IN THE NOVELS OF GEORGE ELIOT,
        THOMAS HARDY AND HENRY JAMES (London:
        Cambridge University Press, 1978), pp. 70–96

        Discusses GE's version of "pathetic tragedy" in *Adam Bede*; of
        the pathetic transformed into "unqualified tragedy" in *The Mill
        on the Floss*; and of heroic tragedy and exceptional individuals in
        The Spanish Gypsy, Felix Holt and *Daniel Deronda*. Contrasts
        GE's and Hardy's conception of tragedy.

132   Caserio, Robert
        PLOT, STORY, AND THE NOVEL: FROM DICKENS AND
        POE TO THE MODERN PERIOD (Princeton: Princeton
        University Press, 1979)

        In a study of the nature and significance of "plot", which
        Caserio values more than most contemporary critics, GE
        receives significant treatment. GE's concern with the inner lives

of characters tends to minimize plot, and allows reduction of action to increase depth of insight and vision.

133   Garrett, Peter K.
THE VICTORIAN MULTIPLOT NOVEL: STUDIES IN DIALOGICAL FORM (New Haven, Conn.: Yale University Press, 1980), pp. 135–79

Treats the Victorian novel as characteristically embodying several plots, playing off against each other and thus resisting determinate meaning. *Middlemarch* offers a "masterfully controlled interplay of perspectives", *Deronda* "radical instability". The multiplot novel is a dialogical form, playing personal narratives against collective perspectives.

134   Stone, Donald D.
THE ROMANTIC IMPULSE IN VICTORIAN FICTION (Cambridge, Mass. and London: Harvard University Press, 1980)

GE's novels represent the climax of the Romantic impulse in Victorian fiction since she has a deep knowledge of the Romantic tradition of several cultures. Analyses the fiction to show how, against her own moral restraints and guilts about fiction writing, and her attempts to purge her characters of their romantic longing, "her own yearning after a means of Romantic apotheosis and self-transcendence intensified with each novel she wrote."

135   Wilt, Judith
GHOSTS OF THE GOTHIC (Princeton: Princeton University Press, 1980), pp. 173–230

Finding "ghosts of the Gothic" in realist narratives, Wilt says that in GE "the sublime thrusts constantly at the common", erupting through what seems banal and ordinary. The novels and protagonists are or become richly aware of the "roar which lies on the other side of silence". Fear and dread in the novels are the means to moral heroism, opening the sublime in the midst of the ordinary. A sensitive reading of the fiction finding Gothic elements that are deeply linked to GE's entire project and to the moral issues of the novels.

136   Joseph, Gerhard
"The *Antigone* as Cultural Touchstone: Matthew Arnold,
Hegel, George Eliot, Virginia Woolf, and Margaret Drabble",
PMLA, 96 (1981), 22–35

Joseph considers Arnold's assessment of the irrelevance of the
Antigone. He refers to GE's essay, "The Antigone and its
Moral", in which she argues for the play's modernity in its
representation of the "struggle between elemental tendencies",
and he examines parallels to the *Antigone* in *The Mill on the
Floss, Middlemarch* and *Romola.*

137   Levine, George
THE REALISTIC IMAGINATION: ENGLISH FICTION
FROM FRANKENSTEIN TO LADY CHATTERLEY
(Chicago: University of Chicago Press, 1981), pp. 252–316

Includes two chapters directly concerned with GE. Considers her
in the context of the developments in realism in nineteenth-
century fiction and in relation to Conrad in particular. Focuses
primarily on *Middlemarch* and *Daniel Deronda* in order to show
how the limits of Victorian realism are extended if not broken, in
part by a reading of nineteenth-century science, in part by the
attempt to face certain irrational elements normally repressed by
realism.

(COMPARISON)

138   Miller, D.A.
NARRATIVE AND ITS DISCONTENTS: PROBLEMS OF
CLOSURE IN THE TRADITIONAL NOVEL (Princeton:
Princeton University Press, 1981), pp. 107–94

Devotes a long chapter to George Eliot. Treats *Middlemarch*
primarily, in the context of a complex argument about the way
narrative and closure are in tension. A very subtle and original
reading of *Middlemarch,* demonstrating how GE averts finality
in crucial scenes normally taken to signify closure.

(MIDDLEMARCH)

139   Qualls, Barry
THE SECULAR PILGRIM OF VICTORIAN FICTION
(Cambridge: Cambridge University Press, 1981), pp. 139–88

A reading primarily from the point of view of novelists' efforts to create a new mythology, based in Bunyan, Quarles and then Carlyle. The treatment of George Eliot sensitively explores the attempt to avoid the diagram for the picture. Qualls gives minute attention to the texts, and reveals a wide knowledge of them and of the Bible and Bunyan, in particular. He thus illuminates the major texts and at the same time gives a sense of the large mythic patterns of GE's work. He reads GE to examine the "themes, situations, and narrative devices that constitute GE's meditations on nineteenth-century English life".

140   Torgovnick, Marianna
       CLOSURE IN THE NOVEL (Princeton: Princeton University Press, 1981), pp. 13–38

       Chapter 1 examines the aesthetic and philosophical integrity of *Middlemarch's* "Finale", which reflects GE's vacillation between being a popular or a philosophical novelist. She converts and integrates the popular convention of "after-history" into an "appropriate end to her intellectual and philosophical novel".

141   Sadoff, Dianne F.
       MONSTERS OF AFFECTION: DICKENS, ELIOT AND BRONTË ON FATHERHOOD (Baltimore: Johns Hopkins University Press, 1982)

       Through the application of sophisticated modern tools of psychoanalysis and semiotics (e.g. Lacan and Kristéva), Sadoff studies "fatherhood" as a symbolic structure. Fatherhood, she argues, is a set of metaphors for subjectivity, and through these metaphors she connects fatherhood with other crucial issues, like class, self-consciousness, sexual difference. Sadoff sees GE as working out of one of the century's dominant images of "fatherhood" — the vision of the father who abandons his children but who remains lovable. Sadoff finds that the ideal authority that GE seeks and tries to impose is a version of her image of the seductive father, requiring passivity before the law; yet at the same time GE subverts by irony the egotism of many of her father figures (Casaubon, e.g. even Savonarola).

142   Wiesenfarth, Joseph
       "The Greeks, The Germans, and George Eliot", *Browning*

Institute Studies, ed. Gerhard Joseph (New York: City University of New York, 1982), pp. 91–104

The essay begins with a useful survey of criticism that has dealt with GE and the classics, and German interpreters of the classics. "Scholarship has demonstrated . . . a nexus involving the Greeks, the Germans, and GE". The essay is then devoted to an exploration of chapter 19 of *Middlemarch,* "perhaps the most allusive chapter in GE".

(MIDDLEMARCH)

143   Carroll, David
      "The Sybil of Mercia", *Studies in the Novel,* 15 (1983), 10–23

Investigates GE's reputation as "Sybil", its sources and its appropriateness. Intelligently points first to her appearance, social circumstances and unusual intelligence. GE seemed a bit frightening in her violation of norms, her "unfeminine" intelligence, her (interpretably) masculine looks. She alarmed and unnerved some, developed worshippers among others, and because of her "improper" social position, she was deprived of normal social intercourse. But GE had an intrinsic instinct to be a sage, which was always partly subverted by her distrust of formulae and by her need to confirm ideas against the human pulses and individual conditions.

144   Hochman, Baruch
      THE TEST OF CHARACTER: FROM THE VICTORIAN NOVEL TO THE MODERN (Rutherford, N.J.: Fairleigh Dickinson University Press; London: Associated University Presses, 1983), pp. 50–71

Looks at GE from the perspective of "the pivotal issue of parents and children, and its moral, psychological, and artistic ramifications". Hochman regards this as the less apparent and more important of GE's concerns in novels that seem to be about egoism and empathy. The tension between childish, demanding characters and motherly ones "to a considerable extent defines the underlying dynamic of GE's work". Hochman perpetuates and elaborates the idea that GE's dominant concern is the need for love. GE's attempt at a normative world is undercut by her need, which polarizes the patterns of her fictions. She manages to mediate those impulses only in *Middlemarch.*

145   Ermarth, Elizabeth
        REALISM AND CONSENSUS IN THE ENGLISH NOVEL
        (Princeton: Princeton University Press, 1983), pp. 222–56

In her chapter on GE, Ermarth emphasizes the way community
in GE is a fundamental condition of meaning, a creation of
many consciousnesses. Consciousness of an objective world is
also consciousness of subjectivity. The objective is the
"correlative result of human agreements". And the agreements
are "accessible" through the "intentional objects that culture
has produced". We are redeemed from solipsism by the social
nature of consciousness. Otherness becomes available through
individuals and individual objects. Difference is form,
separation a precondition for joining together. In the novels,
recognizing difference is a condition for breaking out of stasis
into sympathy, which in GE doesn't mean giving up the self, but
recognizing it.

146   Graver, Suzanne
        "Modeling Natural History: George Eliot's Framings of the
        Present", *Studies in the Novel,* 15 (1983), 26–34

GE confronts the present, which, in the evolutionary model, is
the resultant condition of gradual change, by setting her novels
in the past. The novels' frames have openings that draw attention
to settings in the past and closings that contain images of change.

147   Chase, Karen
        EROS AND PSYCHE: THE REPRESENTATION OF
        PERSONALITY IN CHARLOTTE BRONTË, CHARLES
        DICKENS, AND GEORGE ELIOT (London: Methuen, 1984),
        pp. 136–87

An original and tactful argument about the way psychological
conceptions of characters generate tensions and therefore
narratives, with their peculiar structures. In her treatment of GE,
Chase focuses on the way "desires" are primary conditions, and
the narratives are structured out of the attempt of characters
(and narrator) to find conscious formulations (often
justifications) of their aims and motives. GE tries to make us see
behaviour from the perspective of the characters and yet to
provide a "superpersonal, scientific and objective explanation".

148   Gallagher, Catherine

THE INDUSTRIAL REFORMATION OF ENGLISH FICTION, 1832–1867 (Chicago: University of Chicago Press, 1985), pp. 237–67

The discussion of GE is part of a complex analysis of the nature of Victorian realism and its relation to social developments. It regards GE as developing a deep anxiety about the object of representation and traces her increasing resistance to representation. In *Felix Holt* we se the disruption of GE's faith in the moral value of representing the social; a discontinuity between facts and values becomes one of the dominant qualities of a later realism.

(FELIX HOLT)

149   Hardy, Barbara
       "George Eliot", FORMS OF FEELING IN VICTORIAN FICTION (London: Methuen, 1985), pp. 131–57

A detailed analysis of the many ways George Eliot represents feeling in her novels. The focus is on such matters as personification and figural language, on character and structure. Hardy discriminates the methods used in pre-*Middlemarch* fiction from those of the later books, and shows how intensely particular moments of feeling are generalized and filled with larger significance.

150   McGowan, John P.
       REPRESENTATION AND REVELATION: VICTORIAN REALISM FROM CARLYLE TO YEATS (Columbia: University of Missouri Press, 1986), pp. 132–57

Argues that "Eliot moves from a simple realism of matching words to a world in *The Mill on the Floss* to a more complex realism, one that envisions the world and converts readers to that world's reality".

Studies of George Eliot's Critical Essays

(See 49, Stange)

151   Strachan, L.R.M.
       "George Eliot as Reviewer", *Notes and Queries,* 174 (1938), 14

       Lists GE's critical contributions to the *Westminster Review.*

152   Rust, James D.
       "George Eliot's Reviews of Three Victorian Poets", *Papers of the Michigan Academy of Science, Arts, and Letters,* 36 (1950), 293–303

       Discusses GE's reviews of Arnold, Tennyson and Browning.

153   Rust, James D.
       "George Eliot on the *Blithedale Romance*", *Boston Public Library Quarterly,* 7 (1955), 207–15

       Attributes the essay to GE. In it she criticizes Hawthorne for failure to develop plot as well as character or to see the characters in a community context.

                                             (COMPARISON)

154   Haight, Gordon S.
       "George Eliot's Theory of Fiction", *Victorian Newsletter,* No. 10 (1956), 1–3

       Bases discussion on GE's *Westminster Review* essays and on items 151, 152 and 155.

155   Rust, James D.
       "The Art of Fiction in George Eliot's Reviews", *Review of English Studies,* 7 (1956), 164–72

       Examines how GE's reviews embody her theory of art, which is that the moral mission of art is to widen our sympathies and that morally and aesthetically successful art tells the truth about life.

156 Stang, Richard
"The Literary Criticism of George Eliot", *PMLA,* 72 (1957),
952–61

An important early study of the way GE's ideas about fiction and
its relation to her major intellectual and aesthetic concerns were
expressed in the journalism she wrote for the *Westminster
Review* and other journals, before she began writing *Scenes of
Clerical Life.*

157 Stang, Richard
THE THEORY OF THE NOVEL IN ENGLAND, 1850–1870
(New York: Columbia University Press; London: Routledge &
Kegan Paul, 1959)

This important survey of attitudes toward fiction in mid-
nineteenth-century England entails extensive discussion of GE,
whose highly developed theories Stang finds representative of
the period as a whole. Stang discusses in particular the notion of
the novelist as having a sacred moral responsibility to the public,
the moral aesthetic, realism and many formal matters, all of
which are relevant to GE's work, even where her theories are not
discussed directly.

158 Roazen, Deborah Heller
"George Eliot and Wordsworth: 'The Natural History of
German Life' and Peasant Psychology", *Research Studies
Washington State University,* 41 (1973), 166–78

Details the ways in which "through her discussion of Riehl's
work on the German peasantry GE arrived at some general
conclusions about peasant life and traits" that recall
Wordsworth but more strongly anticipate "her own fuller
fictional treatment of such subjects".

(COMPARISON)

159 Myers, William
"George Eliot's Essays and Reviews", *Prose Studies,* 1 (1978),
5–20

Takes off from Nietzsche's critique of GE for sustaining
Christian morality unquestioningly without the Christian God,

looking in the early reviews for her views in the issue. The early writings "affirm the legitimacy of her break with Orthodox Christianity". The major essays, 1854–1857, are excellent at "the special case", weak in handling "large views and generalizations". The essay analyses GE's organicist conception of society and her political conservatism, and her bringing together of realism with moral feeling. Her criticism reveals a mixture of toughness and oversimplifying efforts at sympathy, and a power of original and creative solutions to problems too frequently handled evasively.

160   Robbins, Bruce
"The Butler Did It: On Agency in the Novel", *Representations,* 6 (Spring, 1984), 85–97

Taking off from GE's painful little essay of 1865, "Servants' Logic", Robbins gets to some central problems in GE's work. The attitudes of that essay reflect both GE's faith in the rationality of history and a serious doubt about the way class divisions challenge the validity of that faith in the gradual teleological movement towards reason. GE considers the possibility that servants' logic is indeed logical, but an alternative logic to our own. The contest between the logics, especially on the issue of causality, is "surprisingly pertinent" to the controversies between Marxism and post-structuralism. Robbins examines *Felix Holt,* and attempts to reconcile "agency" and "meaning" in that work and in the GE canon.

(FELIX HOLT)

Feminism and Feminist Criticism

(See also Showalter in 49)

161   Basch, Françoise
        RELATIVE CREATURES: VICTORIAN WOMEN IN
        SOCIETY AND THE NOVEL, 1837–67, trans. Anthony
        Rudolf (New York: Schocken Books, 1974)

        GE figures importantly in this work, although only *Adam Bede*
        receives extensive discussion (in relation to the theme of
        "seduction"). Basch argues that female figures in the Victorian
        novel, unlike contemporary fictional figures on the Continent,
        or her own predecessors in England, are simple, caricatured. GE
        offers a transition from the Victorian stereotypes of the "wife-
        mother" and the characters of self-conscious feminists.

162   Beer, Patricia
        "READER, I MARRIED HIM": A STUDY OF THE
        WOMEN CHARACTERS OF JANE AUSTEN,
        CHARLOTTE BRONTË, ELIZABETH GASKELL AND
        GEORGE ELIOT (London: Macmillan, 1974), pp. 175–213

        "Of the four writers . . . GE has the highest faith in the
        potential of women and the deepest distrust in the likelihood of
        its negation". *The Spanish Gyspy* is the work in which is most
        clearly expressed the view that woman is capable of high quests
        of lofty importance. Analyses the novels with a view to clarifying
        GE's sense of that possibility and her strong sense of the
        constricting and inhibiting forces, both social and psychological.

163   Austen, Zelda
        "Why Feminist Critics are Angry with George Eliot", *College
        English,* 37 (1976), 549–61

        Summarizes feminist critical discussion of GE and defines the
        limits of GE's feminism. Showalter (in 49) discusses why GE —
        "Sister George" — belongs importantly to the feminist tradition
        in spite of feminist critiques which include Kate Millett's and
        Ellen Moers'.

164   Calder, Jenni
        WOMEN AND MARRIAGE IN VICTORIAN FICTION
        (London: Thames & Hudson, 1976), pp. 121–58

Despite aloofness to "causes", GE had a "natural sympathy
with the women's movement". After a brief sketch of GE's life
in relation to family, work and women, Calder reads GE in
contrast to Linton and Elizabeth Gaskell. "If it seems that in
GE's novels the ultimate answer is very often retreat and
compromise, whereas in her own life she did neither, this may
reflect her own very intimate understanding of the difficulties".
Calder tries to trace this understanding and GE's place in the
women's movement through a reading of the novels,
emphasizing placement of the characters within communities,
and their capacity for passion. GE, however, "does not commit
herself fully to the energies and aspirations she lets loose" in her
heroines.

165   Moers, Ellen
        LITERARY WOMEN (New York: Doubleday, 1976)

Interested in women's tradition in writing, Moers finds Jane
Austen behind GE's development as a novelist: GE "turned her
childhood memories into fiction by turning *Emma* inside out".
Adam Bede is, as it were, addressed to *Emma,* taking the
marginal figures of Austen's novel and making them central.
Mme de Staël and George Sand are also important influences.
GE figures importantly throughout this book, although there are
few extended passages about her.

166   Showalter, Elaine
        A LITERATURE OF THEIR OWN: BRITISH WOMEN
        NOVELISTS FROM BRONTË TO LESSING (Princeton:
        Princeton University Press, 1977)

This groundbreaking book in feminist criticism treats GE
intermittently throughout, although she is not a focus of
attention. Showalter emphasizes the effective influence of GE on
women writers while at the same time demonstrating the
inadequacy of the criticism that insists on a "great tradition",
which in effect ignores all but a very few women writers and
overemphasizes the influence of the more famous ones on each
other.

167   Zimmerman, Bonnie S.
"'Radiant as a Diamond': George Eliot, Jewelry and the Female
Role", *Criticism,* 19 (1977), 212–22

Explores GE's use of jewelry as a metaphor to contest the role of
woman as vain, ornamental sexual object with her role as wife
and mother in *Adam Bede, Middlemarch* and *Daniel Deronda.*
Jewelry becomes an emblem of woman's struggle to transform
her life.

168   Gilbert, Sandra and Gubar, Susan
THE MADWOMAN IN THE ATTIC: THE WOMAN
WRITER AND THE NINETEENTH-CENTURY
LITERARY IMAGINATION (New Haven, Conn.: Yale
University Press, 1979)

Takes "The Lifted Veil" as symptomatic of GE's attitude
toward the Romantic tradition and earlier women writers like
Brontë and Mary Shelley, and their influence on her other more
famous characters, and "on the tensions that continued to
inform her life in spite of her successful writing career". Latimer
is in a sense a female, "a paradigmatic second-born child who
must resort to passivity and invalidism to survive", and his story
is about the problem of a woman writer whose womanhood
impedes her power to write. "Eliot experiences her own anger as
potentially murderous", and in her novels she becomes an
"Angel of Destruction". Extended analysis of several novels
reveals the interrelation betwen the commitment to renunciation
and the passion for destruction.

169   Levine, George
"Repression and Vocation in George Eliot: A Review Essay",
Women and Literature, 7 (1979), 3–13

Levine considers the inadequacy of a strictly psychological
analysis of GE's work, arguing that to understand its full
feminist implications it is necessary to read the characters in
terms of the social pressures upon them. The alternative to
repression is a true vocation, and the question of self-denial is
complicated by what constitutes vocation. "GE's determination
that her work be judged as a man's is in the end an expression of
her ambitious demand for the sanctioning of her own vocation".

170   Greenstein, Susan M.
         "The Question of Vocation: from *Romola* to *Middlemarch*",
         Nineteenth Century Fiction, 35 (1981), 487–505

Considers GE's concern with vocation in the light of her place in the feminist tradition she was rather reluctant to claim. Greenstein sees *Romola* as the first and most explicit "diagramming of the vocational crisis". *Romola* examines the question of vocation in the confines of the family, while *Middlemarch* examines it in terms of the larger society.

171   Knoepflmacher, U.C.
         "Unveiling Men: Power and Masculinity in George Eliot's Fiction", MEN BY WOMEN, ed. Janet Todd (New York: Holmes and Meier, 1981), pp. 130–46.

"GE's attempts to liberate a stifled or veiled female self are primarily enacted through her handling of male characters — her own projections on and impersonations of, a masculinity she wants to tame, subdue, or feminize". Women tend to remain impenetrable and mysterious (consider Latimer's powers, except with Bertha). GE's own ambivalence towards family and then friends led her to give women fulfilment through men: "it hardly seems surprising that her fiction offers what is probably the richest and most variegated cast of male characters created by any woman novelist". GE tries to avoid romance, fantasy imagination of woman's power, as in Charlotte Brontë, yet the end of *The Mill on the Floss* is by "a female fantasist who chafes at the restrictions imposed on her . . .". GE punishes men when they are excessively "phallic", but more normally chastens them by transferring to them the deprivations and sufferings of women, or redeems them through women. A third class of men are "half-feminine". GE found that through men she could liberate female imagination, and thus, much more than their female counterparts, her male characters are subjected to a relentless process of transformation.

172   Brownstein, Rachel M.
         BECOMING A HEROINE: READING ABOUT WOMEN IN NOVELS (New York: Viking Press, 1982)

As part of a deftly autobiographical critical study of the novelistic tradition of the heroine, Brownstein devotes a long chapter to *Daniel Deronda,* but the book is strewn with miscellaneous allusions to the major novels, as well. The overall argument is that the tradition of the heroine gives women a shape for their ambition to move beyond the restrictions of their lives.

173   Goode, John
"The Affections Clad with Knowledge: Women's Duty and the Public Life", *Literature and History*, 9 (1983), 38–51

Goode explores the paradox of GE's relation to fiction writing. She claimes to want a woman's work, and retreats from the "male" position with the *Westminster Review* to a more acceptable woman's occupation: "Writing novels may be a good compromise between the vocations of intellectual leadership and womanhood". As fiction writer, GE can "participate in the social captainship". Goode talks mostly about *Romola, Daniel Deronda* and *The Mill on the Floss,* the latter's awareness of sexual politics being so high that it requires a new kind of realism. Goode argues that GE's awareness of the problems extends her beyond even the most advanced discussion of her day.

174   Edwards, Lee
PSYCHE AS HERO: FEMALE HEROISM AND FICTIONAL FORM (Middletown, Conn.: Wesleyan University Press, 1984)

In the course of an ambitious study aimed at revising Gilbert and Gubar (167), Edward treats *Middlemarch* as part of a longer argument. There is a tradition of heroism which transcends gender, which is available to women as well as men because heroism does not depend on sheer physical prowess. The woman "hero" mounts a direct attack on patriarchy, unlike the heroines of indirection or submission, and even on the traditions of heroism associated with the male. The hero aspires, and aspiration is, Edwards says, " a human necessity". The woman hero exposes fractures in social organization, strips away disguise, overtly, radically, attacks. In this scheme *Middlemarch* is found lacking. Dorothea is limited not simply by the structures of society, but by GE's lack of sympathy for her aspirations. Dorothea Brooke inspires imagination of heroic possibility, but she is transformed by GE into a heroine.

175   Beer, Gillian
GEORGE ELIOT (Brighton: Harvester Press, 1986)

As part of a series on "Key Women Writers", this volume offers a feminist perspective on GE, addressing the problem of why GE has not fared well among modern feminists. Beer insists that any theory that cannot take into account an achievement as impressive as GE's must be inadequate, and she goes on to read GE's life and fictions in the light of feminist issues, of contemporary opinion and social context, and of modern feminist theory.

176   Homans, Margaret
        BEARING THE WORD: LANGUAGE AND FEMALE EXPERIENCE IN NINETEENTH-CENTURY WOMEN'S WRITING (Chicago: University of Chicago Press, 1986), pp. 120–52; 189–222

Includes two chapters primarily devoted to GE. Homans takes two Wordsworth poems, "Tintern Abbey" and "Nutting", both of which conclude with the poet's address to a sister, and considers GE's version of them: "What is the female listener . . . to do with these words that are intended to help her circumvent the painful experience that have forged the poet's consciousness? What does it mean to follow instruction not for the sake of the student but for the sake of the teacher? . . . These are not Wordsworth's concern, but they are Eliot's". Homans argues that gender difference is the basis of GE's ambivalent response to Wordsworth.

Philosophy and Religion

(See Vogeler in 49)

177   Brown, John Crombie
       THE ETHICS OF GEORGE ELIOT'S WORKS (Philadelphia:
       George H. Buchanan and Co., 1885)

       Reads GE as a moralist and studies each novel as a narrative of
       Christian self-sacrifice. Thus GE is a great expositor of Christian
       ethics.

178   Royce, Josiah
       "George Eliot as a Religious Teacher", FUGITIVE ESSAYS
       (Cambridge, Mass.: Harvard University Press, 1925), pp.
       261–89

       The famous American philospher discusses philosophical
       influences on GE, but emphasizes that she was artist, not
       philospher, and that her deep scepticism kept her from
       commitment to abstract formulae.

179   Pond, E.J.
       LES IDÉES MORALES ET RELIGIEUSES DE GEORGE
       ELIOT (Paris: Les Presses Universitaires, 1927)

       Written as a thesis at the University of Lille, this book studies the
       importance and beauty of GE's moral ideas, their relation to the
       other elements that go into the composition of her art. A first
       chapter provides a biographical sketch of GE's youth, and a
       second chapter defines the dominant traits of her nature in
       narrating the major formative events of her later life. Chapter 3
       traces the influence of important writers (predominantly French)
       on her thought. The central fourth chapter is devoted to the
       "teachings" in her novels. Pond also compares GE to other
       Victorian writers and considers the way she has been regarded by
       French critics.

180   House, Humphrey
       "Qualities of George Eliot's Unbelief", IDEAS AND BELIEFS
       OF THE VICTORIANS (London: Sylvan Press, 1949), pp.
       157–63

Discusses GE's movement from Evangelicalism to unbelief and her odd place within Victorian society. Points out that in Marian Evans' study of the early church she found that it was often corrupt, and that in her relation to Hennell and Bray she learned to see all apparent miracles as resolvable into natural events. For GE Christianity lost its historical basis "but it remained the most relevant and moving symbolism for the mysteries of life".

181   Willey, Basil
        NINETEENTH CENTURY STUDIES (London: Chatto and Windus; New York: Columbia University Press, 1949; repr. New York: Harper and Row, 1966)

In two influential chapters, focusing, as the title of the first chapter notes, on "George Eliot: Hennell, Strauss and Feuerbach", Willey discusses GE's secular beliefs, the positivism and humanism she learned from the Brays and Hennells, and the European writers she read and translated. Willey emphasizes the pessimistic implications of her humanism.

182   Svaglic, Martin J.
        "Religion in the Novels of George Eliot", *Journal of English and Germanic Philology,* 53 (1954), 145–59

Emphasizes how her lost Christianity influenced her humanism and her desire for communal solidarity. Discusses GE's love of the religion she rejected.

183   Niebhur, H. Richard
        "Introduction", THE ESSENCE OF CHRISTIANITY, by Ludwig Feuerbach; trans. GE (New York: Harper & Row, 1957)

Primarily concerned with Feuerbach's argument and Karl Barth's analysis of it rather than with its relation to GE.

184   Maison, Margaret M.
        THE VICTORIAN VISION: STUDIES IN THE RELIGIOUS NOVEL (New York: Sheed & Ward, 1961). [Published in England as *Carry on, Eustace*]

Takes GE as an example of Nonconformist thinking, whose novels work out a Christian doctrine of consequences. Discusses *Scenes of Clerical Life, Adam Bede, Romola.*

185   Levine, George
        "Determinism and Responsibility in the Works of George
        Eliot", *PMLA,* 77 (1962), 268–79

        Demonstrates that George Eliot was a determinist who,
        nevertheless, tried to avoid some of the restricting moral
        implications of determinism — the idea that we are not free to
        choose and act. Emphasizes that, for GE, knowledge and growth
        depend on the law of consequences, that in a determinist world
        everything is interdependent, and that rigorous exercise of the
        will to act on what has been learned is essential for the moral life.
        (PHILOSOPHY)

186   Cockshut, A.O.J.
        THE UNBELIEVERS: ENGLISH AGNOSTIC THOUGHT,
        1840–1890 (London: Collins, 1964), pp. 44–58

        Considers GE's "reverent agnosticism", and concludes that
        "having regretfully concluded that Heavenly Justice was
        incredible, she could not give up a belief in a natural, earthly
        justice, infallible as if it had been divine".

187   Knoepflmacher, U.C.
        "George Eliot, Feuerbach, and the Question of Criticism",
        Victorian Studies, 7 (1964), 306–9

        Suggests that criticism must take into account GE's philosophy if
        it is to do justice to her works. Usefully demonstrates how
        Feuerbachian principles underlie crucial moments in *Adam
        Bede.*

188   Schneewind, Jerome B.
        "Moral Problems and Moral Philosophy in the Victorian
        Period", *Victorian Studies,* 9 (1965), supplement, 29–46

        Attempts to show how understanding a literary work may be
        assisted by an understanding of philosophical issues, focusing on
        the debate between Utilitarians and Intuitionists on ethics.
        Treats *Daniel Deronda* as a novel which deals with "the
        conceptual tension" between an Intuitionist and determinist
        attitude. Deronda's fate works out a reconciliation between
        GE's intuitional morality and determinist sense of the world.

189   Baker, William
GEORGE ELIOT AND JUDAISM, Salzburg Studies in English
Literature (Salzburg: Institut für Englische Sprache und
Literatur, Universität Salzburg, 1975)

A detailed and well-documented volume that traces GE's
relation to Judaism from her earliest readings in the Old
Testament through her later readings in Jewish history and
mysticism. Uses this material for analyses of *Daniel Deronda,*
"The Lifted Veil", *Romola* and *The Spanish Gypsy.*

190   Shaffer, E.S.
"KUBLA KHAN" AND THE FALL OF JERUSALEM: THE
MYTHOLOGICAL SCHOOL IN BIBLICAL CRITICISM
AND SECULAR LITERATURE (London: Cambridge
University Press, 1975), pp. 225–91

An important and difficult essay arguing that GE's formal
innovations are dictated by her moral concerns. Rejecting
critical concern about GE's realism as obfuscating her originality
and her achievement in *Deronda,* Shaffer emphasizes the
relation of Biblical higher criticism to the novel: the novel is part
of a tradition attempting to join East and West, an attempt at "a
cosmopolitan religious epic", and in this book GE "is a
European writer". GE does not attempt to represent realistically
religious experience, but, as in "Amos Barton", showing the
roots of theology and "constructing a carefully controlled vision
of the future of religion". The essay places GE's apparently
over-idealized and sentimental sequences in the context of her
mythic enterprise, bringing poetic and religious techniques
together and demonstrating the impossibility of this synthesis in
an age of criticism.

191   Ashton, Rosemary
THE GERMAN IDEA: FOUR ENGLISH WRITERS AND
THE RECEPTION OF GERMAN THOUGHT, 1800–1860
(Cambridge: Cambridge University Press, 1980)

A study of the stages of the entrance of German philosophy,
history and aesthetics into English thought, focusing on
Coleridge, Carlyle, Lewes and GE. Discusses specifically GE's
translations of Strauss, Spinoza and Feuerbach, and her reading
of Goethe and Heine.

192   Wright, T.R.
        "George Eliot and Positivism", *Modern Language Review,* 76
        (1981), 257–72

Not so much an analysis of how Positivism operates in the novels
as a demonstration that it *does* operate and that from her first
reading of him in 1851 GE admired Comte, and well beyond the
limits criticism following Gordon Haight's biography has been
willing to allow. Wright demonstrates that we must take Comte's
influence and Comte himself very seriously if we are to read the
novels with the kind of understanding we expect. Excellent use of
notebooks, letters, journals.

Science

193   Johnson, M.L.
"George Eliot and George Combe", *Westminster Review,* 156 (1906), 557–68

Argues that George Combe's phrenology exercised a strong influence on GE's thinking and art, and that evidence of that influence is manifest in the fiction.

194   Cazamian, Madeleine L.
LE ROMAN ET LES IDÉES EN ANGLETERRE: L'INFLUENCE DE LA SCIENCE (1860–1890) (Strasbourg: Librairie Istra, 1923), pp. 92–171

An extensive study of GE's work in light of the major philosophic, scientific and religious ideas GE studied and propogated. Beginning with a brief intellectual biography, Cazamian proceeds to discuss GE's relation to the scientific and philosophical thought of her time, and documents her "prodigious" reading and learning. Cazamian relies heavily on GE's own comments in her fiction on realism and science and emphasizes her taste for ideas. She then devotes long sections on determinism to *Adam Bede,* on evolution to *The Mill on the Floss* and *Silas Marner,* on social ideas to *Felix Holt* and *Daniel Deronda,* and on "intuitionism and the religious attitude" in *Middlemarch.* These offer extensive discussions of the deep analytical way GE portrays character and through that portrayal modifies her ideas.

195   Feltes, N.N.
"Phrenology from Lewes to George Eliot", *Studies in the Literary Imagination,* I (1968), 13–22

Discusses the enthusiasm for phrenology, its connection with radical anti-establishment frames of mind, and the movement in Lewes from phrenology to positivism. GE rejected the crude claims of phrenology, but believed in "the real anatomical basis" of mind. Her materialism and her habits of mind were influenced by phrenology, as Feltes shows by brief allusion to the novels.

196   Newton, K.M.
"George Eliot, George Henry Lewes, and Darwinism",
Durham University Journal, 35 (1974), 278–93

GE accepted Darwin's theory but was worried by natural
selection, as dehumanizing, and by the purposelessness of
evolution. Examines Lewes's views, as expressed in his essays,
"Mr Darwin's Hypotheses", that the great achievement of
Darwin is explaining evolution without metaphysics. GE resisted
the attempt to explain society by analogy with the adaptation and
struggle of natural selection. Christian in *Felix Holt* represents a
Darwinian view of individualism, and Darwin in general
intensified GE's exploration of egoism.

197   Alaya, Flavia
"Victorian Science and the 'Genius' of Woman", *Journal of the
History of Ideas,* 38 (1977), 261–80

As an historical movement, feminist philosophical
egalitarianism suffered a setback in the nineteenth century that
had its origin in Victorian science, "which gave vigorous and
pervasive reinforcement to the traditional dogmatic view of
sexual character". GE figures in this essay in only a very minor
way, but it is relevant to her own attitudes towards women.

198   Collins, K.K.
"G.H. Lewes Revised: George Eliot and the Moral Sense",
Victorian Studies, 21 (1978), 463–83

Discusses GE's completion of the last two volumes of Lewes's
Problems of Life and Mind. Despite her sympathies with
Lewes's views, she differed in many ways and "subtly
reformulated a number of points". Collins concentrates on GE's
attempt to assert her own "individualistic conception of duty",
and describes the similarity of her moral perceptions as revealed
in her revisions of Lewes's work to the moral perceptions of her
own fiction.

199   Beer, Gillian
"Plot and the Analogy with Science in Later Nineteenth-
Century Novelists", *Comparative Criticism,* 2 (1980), 131–49

Not primarily about GE, this essay locates her and *Middlemarch* in nineteenth-century scientific discussion. The metaphors of science carry over into fiction, and the problem of determinism, the individual constrained by laws of nature, was addressed by some new scientific experimental procedures. Science was throwing all stable things and categories into time, and scientific truth "is expressible only as relations". Beer examines in particular the uses of analogy in science and in *Middlemarch* as ways to help make sense of an overwhelmingly complex world.

200   Levine, George
"George Eliot's Hypothesis of Reality", *Nineteenth-Century Fiction,* 35 (1980), 1–28

GE's determination to listen closely and to open herself to knowledge and to extend sympathy to others is related to her sense of what good science is. Through extensive comparison of Lewes's *Problems of Life and Mind* with GE's work, particularly *Daniel Deronda* and *Middlemarch,* this essay suggests the importance for GE's aesthetic and moral positions of her understanding and knowledge of science.

201   Cosslett, Tess
THE SCIENTIFIC MOVEMENT AND VICTORIAN LITERATURE (Brighton: Harvester Press, 1982)

GE's novels reflect the Victorian scientific world view sketched by Cosslett in the earlier part of the book: e.g. gradualism, cause-and-effect, empiricism. The section on GE reviews well-known passages, particularly the passage about Lydgate's scientific ideals. The scientific model is an ethical one, as well; thus bad behaviour is invariably "unscientific". Science requires both detachment and imaginative searching. Considers, especially, *Middlemarch.*

202   Wright, T.R.
"From Bumps to Morals: the Phrenological Background to George Eliot's Moral Framework", *Review of English Studies,* 33 (1982), 35–46

Sees phrenology as providing a systematic intellectual structure to the novels, and claims that Comte's cerebral theory provides a key to understanding GE's moral framework. Provides a brief history of the development of phrenology, and suggests how Comte's cerebral theory, which emphasized moral rather than anatomical matters, was deeply influential on English thinkers, particularly Lewes. Wright concedes that GE was not an orthodox phrenologist, yet shows that there are many allusions to phrenology in the novel, and that GE copied out Comte's cerebral theory into two of her notebooks.

203   Beer, Gillian
        DARWIN'S PLOTS: EVOLUTIONARY NARRATIVE IN DARWIN, GEORGE ELIOT, AND NINETEENTH-CENTURY FICTION (London: Routledge & Kegan Paul, 1983)

Beer includes two exemplary chapters on GE, applying subtly elaborated aspects of Darwin's theory. GE's commitment to science in *Middlemarch* leads to a new kind of richness: the parallels and sources in science are not discrete passages, but a full engagement with major contemporary enquiries, particularly into nature and evolution. Beer shows how "Darwin's insights and the difficulties raised by those insights move into the substance of the novels' projects", and she shows how the novels struggle with the tensions between individual need and the inexorable "disclosures of law", which is all that remains against Darwin's world of endless change. In her final GE chapter, Beer asks: "Can fiction restore to the female the power of selection which, Darwin held, men had taken over? And can the woman writing shape new future stories?"

(FEMINISM)

204   Shuttleworth, Sally
        GEORGE ELIOT AND NINETEENTH-CENTURY SCIENCE: THE MAKE-BELIEVE OF A BEGINNING (Cambridge: Cambridge University Press, 1984)

Shows how "scientific ideas and theories of method affected not only the social vision but also the narrative structure and fictional methodology" of GE's novels. Focus is on "organicism". Shuttleworth elaborates a contradiction in "organicism" that has important consequences for the novels. The early works, in the empiricist mode of natural history, imply an ahistorical stability, gradualism and continuity. But natural history applied to biological phenomena "requires a conception of continuing and significant change" and such change cannot fit into GE's earlier conception of ahistorical stability in nature. Organicism, while normally associated with conservatism because it implies that any change will have radical implications for the whole organism, also implies that no object remains as it was. This dual vision of the organic — conservative ahistoricism and radical change — informs the narrative experiment in *Daniel Deronda*. The revisionary readings that follow from this view are an important contribution to GE studies.

Comparison of George Eliot with Other Writers

205   Berle, Lina Wright
       GEORGE ELIOT AND THOMAS HARDY: A CONTRAST
       (New York: Michell Kernnerley, 1917; repr. New York:
       Bookfinger, 1969)

       Beginning with lamentation at the breakdown of standards and
       the "exaggerated humanitarianism" that leads writers to focus
       on "our social and intellectual inferiors", Berle finds in GE a
       "rational idealism . . . Humanitarian zeal in GE is qualified by
       a strong recognition of the needs for standards and criteria
       whereby to make effective the attempted reforms". GE is treated
       as a moral and social ideal at a time of decline, as a representative
       of the good "old humanitarianism". Hardy is contrasted as
       representative of the bad "new". The analysis and comparison
       of the works is insistently moralistic.

206   Gary, Franklin
       "In Search of George Eliot: An Approach through Marcel
       Proust", *Symposium,* 4 (1933), 182–206

       A discussion of what Proust admired in GE, particularly her use
       of "memory".

207   Leavis, Q.D.
       "A Note on Literary Indebtedness: Dickens, George Eliot,
       Henry James", *Hudson Review,* 8 (1955), 423–8

       Compares the scenes among the Roman ruins in *Little Dorrit,*
       Middlemarch and *The Portrait of a Lady.* Illuminates important
       differences and relations among the novelists.

208   Stone, Wilfred
       "Hale White and George Eliot", *University of Toronto
       Quarterly,* 25 (1956), 437–51

       Discusses the view of William Hale White ("Mark Rutherford")
       of his relations with GE, with whom he worked in the offices of
       the *Westminster Review.* He was "entirely overcome with

unhesitating absorbing love for her''. Stone argues that the record of White's feelings and relation to GE is in *The Autobiography of Mark Rutherford* and other semi-fictional White writings. An interesting episode in briefly crossing paths of Victorian novelists and intellectuals.

209   Levine, George
"Isabel, Gwendolen, and Dorothea'', *English Literary History,* 30 (1963), 244–57

Indicates how *Portrait of a Lady* is indebted to *Middlemarch* as well as to *Daniel Deronda* (F.R. Leavis's argument). Both GE novels focus on female egoists trapped in loveless marriages, and explore the consequences of choice and the possibilities of freedom much as James was to do.

210   Carroll, David
"*Mansfield Park, Daniel Deronda,* and Ordination'', *Modern Philology,* 62 (1965), 217–26

Examines each novel's similar conflict between the demands of vocation and the demands of self. Through analysis of several passages, Carroll demonstrates GE's indebtedness to Austen and outlines her different assumptions about society and the individual.

211   Duerksen, Roland
"Shelley in *Middlemarch*'', *Keats–Shelley Journal,* 14 (1965), 23–31

Ladislaw in partly based on Shelley, many of whose ideas and characteristics he shares. "There are indications . . . that GE had a better understanding and more genuine appreciation of Shelley as ethical and social thinker than did most of the creative writers of her generation''.

212   Mansell, Jr, Darrell
"Ruskin and George Eliot's 'Realism''', *Criticism,* 7 (1965), 203–16

Argues that neither Ruskin nor GE advocated the "exact imitation of nature''. GE's metaphor of artist as optical instrument is part of an aesthetic theory in which the structure of the novel can be dictated by the process of the author's memory.

213 Knoepflmacher, U.C.
"Of Time, Rivers, and Tragedy: George Eliot and Matthew Arnold", *Victorian Newsletter,* No. 33 (1968), 1–5

Compares GE's derogation of "ordinary novel readers" and her impulse to tragedy in *The Mill on the Floss* to Arnold's position and his work on *Merope*. Compares Latimer of "The Lifted Veil" to Empedocles, and examines the different responses of GE and Arnold to the dark vision of their own works and to their attempts to find the tragic in the ordinary.

214 Hardy, Barbara
"Mrs Gaskell and George Eliot", THE VICTORIANS, HISTORY OF LITERATURE IN THE ENGLISH LANGUAGE, ed. Arthur Pollard (New York: Bantam; London: Cressit, 1969), pp. 169–95

A brief introduction to GE's life and artistic accomplishments, emphasizing the novel's authorial centre, moral dimensions and psychological realism.

215 Smalley, Barbara
GEORGE ELIOT AND FLAUBERT: PIONEERS OF THE MODERN NOVEL (Athens: Ohio University Press, 1974)

Suggests that despite obvious differences, GE and Flaubert have much in common in their work. In particular, Smalley emphasizes the narrative focus on the illusion of characters, like Dorothea Brooke and Emma Bovary, and on the awareness of the writer's predicament. Both GE and Flaubert, in their concern with the psychology of characters, seen against the background of an impersonal world (which functions ironically) anticipate modernist developments in fiction.

216 Beeton, Ridley
"Joseph Conrad and George Eliot: An Indication of the Possibilities", *Polish Review,* 20 (1975), 78–86

Briefly suggests structural and imagistic affinities between *Heart of Darkness* and *Silas Marner, Nostromo* and *Middlemarch;*

Under Western Eyes, affinities "far closer than Leavis' tradition allows".

217   Sullivan, William J.
"George Eliot and Goethe's *Faust*", *George Eliot Fellowship Review,* 6 (1975), 15–22

218   Thomson, Patricia
GEORGE SAND AND THE VICTORIANS: HER INFLUENCE IN NINETEENTH-CENTURY ENGLAND (London: Macmillan, 1977)

Considers the biographical and literary evidence for Sand's influence on GE's life and fiction. Sand's early romantic novels, her confessional writings and her pastoral novels all appealed to GE largely for thematic reasons. Detailed discussion of *The Mill on the Floss;* some discussion of the other novels.

219   McGuinn, Nicholas
"George Eliot and Mary Wollstonecraft", THE NINETEENTH-CENTURY WOMAN: HER CULTURAL AND PHYSICAL WORLD, ed. Sara Delamont and Lorna Duffin (London: Croom Helm; New York: Barnes and Noble, 1978)

Analyses GE's review, "Margaret Fuller and Mary Wollstonecraft", arguing that GE chose to discuss the older *Vindication* with the recent *Women in the Nineteenth Century* in order to "advance the idea of a growing tradition of feminist theory" and "reacquaint the public with the work of Mary Wollstonecraft". However, the language and rhetorical strategy of the review betray GE's unease and reluctance.

(FEMINISM)

220   Beer, Gillian
"Beyond Determinism: George Eliot and Virginia Woolf", WOMEN WRITING AND WRITING ABOUT WOMEN, ed. Mary Jacobus (London: Croom Helm; New York: Barnes and Noble, 1979)

Beer discusses GE's ideas about determinism and ways in which determinism constricts the possibilities open to her characters. Shows how she tries to get around those constrictions, particularly in *Daniel Deronda,* and relates this to Woolf's way of dealing with the same problem.

221   Witemeyer, Hugh
       "George Eliot and Jean-Jacques Rousseau", *Comparative Literature Studies,* 16 (1979), 121–30

Examines the influence of Rousseau on "The Lifted Veil" and *Daniel Deronda.* The latter reflects a "shift in values from self-cultivation to social service" that Wordsworth taught the Victorians.

222   Mann, Karen B.
       "George Eliot and Wordsworth: The Power of Sound and the Power of the Mind", *Studies in English Literature,* 20 (1980), 675–94

In relation to Wordsworth's and GE's metaphors of sound, Mann carefully examines how in "The Legend of Jubal" and in the novels GE re-examines the Romantic concept of imagination as the mind's crucial faculty. Ultimately, GE focuses on the moment when the mind conceives its difference from the outside world whereas for Wordsworth the crucial moment is the mind's recognition of connection.

223   McCobb, Anthony
       GEORGE ELIOT'S KNOWLEDGE OF GERMAN LIFE AND LETTERS (Salzburg: Institut für Anglistik und Amerikanistik, Universität Salzburg, 1982)

Essentially a catalogue of all materials relating to GE's knowledge of German literature and culture. The Introduction traces her visits to Germany and her German reading throughout her career and lets nothing escape. (It also summarizes briefly her reading in English, American, Italian and French writings!) The catalogue itself usefully gathers essential information on GE's reading and her discussions of the reading. Draws on journals, letters of GE and GHL, and additional material when possible.

224   Shaw, Harry E.
       "Scott and George Eliot: The Lure of the Symbolic", SCOTT AND HIS INFLUENCE, ed. David Hewitt and Thomas

Crawford (Aberdeen: Association for Scottish Literary Studies, 1983), pp. 393–402

George Eliot and the Arts

225   Levenson, Shirley Frank
       "The Use of Music in *Daniel Deronda*", *Nineteenth-Century
       Fiction,* 24 (1969), 317–34

       Explores in detail Eliot's unifying uses of music in *Daniel
       Deronda.* Music is associated with the expression of deep feeling
       and with the idealized Jewish characters. It represents an ideal
       Gwendolen can never attain.

226   Murdoch, John
       "English Realism: George Eliot and the Pre-Raphaelites",
       Journal of the Warburg and Cortauld Institutes, 37 (1974),
       313–29

       Murdoch argues for the "intellectual importance of the Realistic
       school in England, especially of the Pre-Raphaelites, who in
       their early years worked out the characteristic minute style that
       dominated visual and literary expression". Traces the distinctive
       qualities of English realism in the Pre-Raphaelites and in GE.

227   Witemeyer, Hugh
       GEORGE ELIOT AND THE VISUAL ARTS (New Haven,
       Conn.: Yale University Press, 1979)

       An original consideration of the relation between GE's work and
       her interest in art. Witemeyer discusses the importance in the
       novels of GE's tendency to describe "scenes", and to see her
       characters and her actions as visual compositions. GE, he points
       out, values the novel over painting, in that the novel can animate
       and render "the truth of change", but she saw pictorialism as a
       necessary if not sufficient condition of her art. Different
       chapters consider history, portrait, landscape and genre
       painting.

228   McCobb, E.A.
       "The Morality of Musical Genius: Schopenhaueran Views in
       Daniel Deronda", *Forum of Modern Language Studies,* 19
       (1983), 321–30

       Shows the overlap of ideas about music in GE and

Schopenhauer. The portrait of Klesmer reflects Schopenhaueran notions of musical genius. McCobb is most interesting, however, in opening remarks that suggest both GE's ambivalence about music as an ethical force, and her tendency to segregate musical achievement sexually, allowing (like Schopenhauer) woman to have talent but not genius. McCobb does not follow up the point that GE's preference for non-verbal public art or for salon or drawing room art contradicts the relatively low value she attaches to it.

The Poetry

(See 11, Paris)

229   James, Henry
Review of *The Spanish Gypsy, Nation,* 7 (1868), 12–14

James expresses deep admiration of *The Spanish Gypsy,* a poem that reveals no new qualities, but that is marvellously crafted, beautiful, and imaginative.

230   James, Henry
"The Spanish Gypsy", *North American Review,* 107 (1868), 620–35

A consideration of the "rhetorical richness" and representation of human character in the poem, which James calls a "romance written by one who is emphatically a thinker".

231   Block, Louis James
"The Poetry of George Eliot", *Sewanee Review,* 26 (1918), 85–91

High praise for the poetry and GE's mastery of poetic form and music. Likens "Jubal" to the grandeur of Dryden's poetry.

232   Newton, K.M.
"Byronic Egoism and George Eliot's *The Spanish Gypsy*", *Neophilologus,* 57 (1973), 388–400

233   Blake, Kathleen
"'Armgart': George Eliot on the Woman Artist", *Victorian Poetry,* 18 (1980), 75–80

Like *Middlemarch* and *Daniel Deronda,* "Armgart" details woman's conflict between love and art, a conflict GE herself evaded but one that expresses the woman artist's embedded ambivalence towards love. In the poems, love and art are reconciled, as they must be, for a woman artist to flourish and succeed.

234 Lisle, Bonnie J.
"Art and Egoism in George Eliot's Poetry", *Victorian Poetry,*
22 (1984), 263—78

Conceding that GE's poetry is second-rate, Lisle nevertheless
argues that it is important for an understanding of her fiction,
and focuses on how the poetry helps us understand why for GE
marriage is "the only happy ending available to her heroines".
Provides a very intelligent reading of "Jubal" and "Armgart",
showing how GE imagines the artist's role. Lisle shows that for
GE "self-annihilation is a debt the artist owes humanity".

(FEMINISM)

235 Neufeldt, Victor A.
"The Madonna and the Gypsy", *Studia Neophilologica* (1983),
44—54

The Spanish Gypsy, not *Romola,* is the turning-point in GE's
career, moving from *Romola* as madonna to Dorothea as wife
and mother through a figure who is angel, goddess, priestess. GE
learns that claims of public duty must not be satisfied at the
expense of personal fulfilment. GE wants to open the possibility
of fulfilment in womanhood rather than complete self-sacrifice.
In *Felix Holt* we get the fusion of public and private good, which
allows GE to finish *The Spanish Gypsy.*

Scenes of Clerical Life

(See Butwin and Carroll in 49; and Oldfield in 47)

236   Tomlinson, May
       "The Beginning of George Eliot's Art: A Study of *Scenes of Clerical Life*", *Sewanee Review,* 27 (1919), 320–9

       An early appreciation of the importance of *Scenes* as work that offers indications of Eliot's talents and ideas, especially of her descriptive observations of nature and of the need for compassion and sympathy.

237   Noble, Thomas A.
       GEORGE ELIOT'S "SCENES OF CLERICAL LIFE" (New Haven, Conn. and London: Yale University Press, 1965)

       Argues that GE's major preoccupations can all be discovered in her first work. After a long discussion of its genesis and publication, Noble describes GE's theory of fiction and discusses the book's implicit worldview, its exemplification of GE's narrative methods, and its foreshadowing of the rest of her work.

238   Knoepflmacher, U.C.
       "George Eliot's Anti-Romantic Romance: 'Mr Gilfil's Love Story'", *Victorian Newsletter,* No. 31 (1967), 11–15

239   Ojha, B.
       "Fiction as Allegory: A Study of 'Janet's Repentance'", *International Journal of English Studies,* 13 (1973), 29–41

       The story is unique in GE's fiction in its attempt to weld spiritual with purely literary values. The success of the first two stories in *Scenes of Clerical Life* emboldened GE to a more daring experiment. Characters and images have an allegorical force that does not diminish the literal realism.

Adam Bede

(See also 46, Creeger)

240   Mottram, William
THE TRUE STORY OF GEORGE ELIOT IN RELATION TO
"ADAM BEDE" GIVING THE REAL LIFE HISTORY OF
THE MORE PROMINENT CHARACTERS (London: F.
Griffiths: T. Fisher Unwin, 1905; rpt. New York: Haskell
House, 1972)

Copious biographical accounts of prototypes of major
characters in *Adam Bede* written by the "Grandnephew of
Adam and Seth Bede and Cousin to the Author".

241   Diekhoff, John S.
"The Happy Ending of *Adam Bede*", *English Literary History*,
3 (1936), 221–7

Diekhoff criticizes the implausibility of the novel's ending,
which GE did not originally intend but which Lewes suggested in
a lapse of judgement. GE's moralizing intrusions, he argues,
make for yet more serious weaknesses.

242   Van Ghent, Dorothy
"Adam Bede", THE ENGLISH NOVEL: FORM AND
FUNCTION (New York: Rinehart, 1953), pp. 171–81

A close reading of the novel, taking off from the narrator's
famous intrusion in chapter 17. GE's veraciousness is to what the
artist sees and is creative rather than passively imitative. The
novel is shaped "through and through by moral judgement and
moral evaluation". Its movement is massively slow, expressive
of the "patient rhythms" of nature, and of the "slow toil" and
discipline that make living valuable.

243   Hussey, Maurice
"Structure and Imagery in *Adam Bede*", *Nineteenth-Century
Fiction*, 10 (1955), 115–29

Studies the novel in terms of its uses of the seasons and the
passage of time. Hussey connects the various changes of seasons

and times with the actions and psychology of the characters, implying that the local time of the narrative suggests a more universal reading.

244   Leavis, F.R.
"Adam Bede", ANNA KARENINA AND OTHER ESSAYS (London: Chatto and Windus, 1970), pp. 49—58

In *Adam Bede* George Eliot is learning how to write a novel. It anticipates her future work and reflects the work of her predecessors like Scott, while Arthur Donnithorne reflects the influence of Hawthorne and Adam reflects Wordsworth. Similarly, Greek tragedy was important to her conception. The novel's greatest historical achievement, however, is in GE's creation of a past England, and her capacity to see dignity in rural characters rooted in community.

245   Martin, Bruce K.
"Rescue and Marriage in *Adam Bede*", *Studies in English Literature,* 12 (1972), 745—63

Martin defends GE's use of rescue and marriage in *Adam Bede,* which is principally concerned with Adam's development of the power of sympathy. The rescue "solves the dilemma posed by a condemned Hetty, just as the marriage helps alleviate the problem of a solitary Adam".

246   Anderson, Roland
"George Eliot Provoked: John Blackwood and Chapter Seventeen of *Adam Bede*", *Modern Philology,* 71 (1973), 39—47

Argues that chapter 17 of *Adam Bede* is GE's direct response to Blackwood's criticisms of *Scenes* and of the early chapters of *Adam Bede*. Blackwood's criticisms and suggestions reveal a preference for popular fictional idealization and didacticism, a preference that finally provoked GE to write her "manifesto" in chapter 17.

247   Adam, Ian
"The Structure of Realisms in *Adam Bede*", *Nineteenth-Century Fiction,* 30 (1975), 127—49

Identifies and discusses in detail three kinds of realistic

procedures used by GE in *Adam Bede:* pictorial realism found in the lavish background; analytic realism, by which historical, sociological and moral reality are explored; and dramatic realism, which engages us in the plights and consciousness of the characters.

248   Herbert, Christopher
"Preachers and the Schemes of Nature in *Adam Bede*", *Nineteenth-Century Fiction,* 29 (1975), 412–27

Adam Bede is rigorously dialectical, affirming the apparent contraries of traditional beliefs and values and positivist and agnostic views. Dinah and Mr Irwine "define the moral and metaphysical issues around which the story revolves". Dinah's sermons are full of latent Calvinist violence; Irwine's gentle tolerance is really "saintly". Dinah rejects "Nature", Irwine accepts it gratefully. His Wordsworthian view is that nature is "inherently sympathetic and beneficial to man". The author, seeing the limits of nature, allies with the Calvinist in attempts to master and transform it. Hetty's story confirms Dinah's Calvinist reading. But the "dialectic" of the novel does not resolve the antithesis between the pastoral ideal of value GE aspires to and the moralist revulsion from nature.

249   Sadoff, Dianne F.
"Nature's Language: Metaphor in the Text of *Adam Bede*", *Genre,* 11 (1978), 411–26

Sadoff argues that *Adam Bede* reveals GE's longing for the transcendental, which creates an irresolvable tension between transcendence and realism. Examines the ways in which figurative language creates and reveals that tension and how GE's "'Language of Nature' deconstructs the text's assertions of coherence, stability, and symbolic unity".

250   Clayton, Jay
"Visionary Power and Narrative Form: Wordsworth and *Adam Bede*", *English Literary History,* 6 (1979), 645–72

The Wordsworthian principle of compensation structures the plot and narrative of the novel. Clayton argues that for his loss of love for Hetty, Adam is compensated by growth into "full consciousness". Similarly, the narrative opens in hard strength, undergoes a crisis of visionary power, and moves to an order in which feeling and consciousness are greater than "the stern logic of consequences".

251   Harris, Simon
"Infanticide and Respectability: Hetty Sorrel as Abandoned Child in *Adam Bede*", *English Studies in Canada,* 9 (1983), 177–96

Examines relation of Hetty to the whole structure of *Adam Bede*. Hetty is one of the most convincing depictions of fallen woman in Victorian literature. There is no polarity between Hetty and Hayslope. Her defects reflect Hayslope's failure and excessive insistence on respectability. She produces Poysers' value without feeling for community. The novel is no mere nostalgic dream of community but the story of three confused orphans who must grow beyond the limits of their class. The conclusion of the novel without Hetty is a denial of all that precedes.

252   Malcom, David
"*Adam Bede* and the Unions: 'a proletarian novel'", *Zeit für Anglistik und Amerikanistic,* 31 (1983), 5–16

Argues that the novel is concerned by indirection with the industrial transformation in England. The treatment of Methodism, of the artisan, of the commercial intrusions on feudal economy, would have had great resonance in the 1850s when the problems of unionization, of the artisan's position, and of dissent's connection with industrialism were prominent. GE "uses issues of the past to deal with issues of the present" and looks critically at the old order.

The Mill on the Floss

(See also 46, Creeger: and 47, Martin, and Hardy in 47)

253 Tomlinson, May
    "Dodsons and Tullivers", *Sewanee Review,* 26 (1918), 319–27

    Tomlinson maintains that the novel's pervasive ironic humour mediates pathos and allows a detachment that rescues it from the dreariness of its exposition of small-mindedness, and of the misery it causes.

254 Steinhoff, William R.
    "Intent and Fulfillment in the Ending of *The Mill on the Floss*", THE IMAGE OF THE WORK: ESSAYS IN CRITICISM, ed. Bertram Evans, Josephine Miles and William R. Steinhoff (Berkeley: University of California Press, 1955), pp. 231–51

    Argues that the ending is well prepared for and symbolically appropriate.

255 Drew, Elizabeth
    "George Eliot: *The Mill on the Floss*", THE NOVEL: A GUIDE TO FIFTEEN MODERN MASTERPIECES (New York: Dell Publishing Co., 1963), pp. 127–40

    An introductory discussion, describing GE's way of revealing character and depicting social background. GE's weakness in melodrama and occasional lapses from plausibility do not "invalidate the sureness and truth of GE's large human understanding".

256 Levine, George
    "Intelligence as Deception: *The Mill on the Floss*", *PMLA,* 80 (1965), 402–9

    Argues that the aspects of the novel normally considered weaknesses are in fact intellectually coherent with the entire carefully thought through structure and philosophical — positivist and humanist — implications of the novel. The intellectual thoroughness disguised from GE the painful revelations her own intelligence had led her to dramatize.

257   Colby, Robert A.
"*The Mill on the Floss:* Maggie Tulliver and the Child of Nature", FICTION WITH A PURPOSE: MAJOR AND MINOR NINETEENTH-CENTURY NOVELS (Bloomington: Indiana University Press, 1967), pp. 213–55

Discusses GE's novel in the context of Victorian "school novels", emphasizing the importance of Wordsworth to writers concerned with child development. Like *The Prelude, The Mill on the Floss* explores the interaction between sensory experience and the sensitive mind and traces the persistence of childhood memories and associations. (Colby's book includes a chapter on *Middlemarch*.)

258   Milner, Ian
"The Quest for Community in *The Mill on the Floss*", *Prague Studies in English,* 12 (1967), 77–92

Locates a conflict of values in the novel, a tension between the need for personal love of family and lover, and the need for community. Against traditional criticism, Milner argues that Stephen is an effective and appropriate character, the first to arouse Maggie's strongly passionate nature. GE allows the sensual element fuller play than in any of the other novels. The conclusion sidesteps Maggie's real quest, for a moral community.

259   Paris, Bernard
"The Inner Conflicts of Maggie Tulliver: A Horneyan Analysis", *Centennial Review,* 13 (1969), 166–99

Attempts to read the novel in the light of Horney's *Neurosis and Growth: The Struggle Toward Self-Realization,* and recants on the judgements in his early work rejecting Leavis's view that Maggie is immature and that her lack of self-knowledge is shared with GE (see 102). Paris admires the portrait of Maggie but disagrees with GE's interpretation of it. Maggie adopts "the extreme form of the self-effacing solution", which is a way to death. The novel brilliantly creates the character, but falsely endorses it as healthy. GE cannot give us the kind of novel she wants to write because she lacks the emotional maturity necessary for it.

260   Moldstad, David

"The Mill on the Floss and *Antigone"*, *PMLA,* 85 (1970), 527–31

Noting that in her essay, "The Antigone and its Moral", GE discusses the play's conflict between the individual's moral vision and society's conventions and that *The Mill on the Floss* does the same thing, Moldstad considers the similarities between *Antigone* and *The Mill on the Floss.*

(COMPARISON)

261   Hagan, John
"A Reinterpretation of *The Mill on the Floss"*, *PMLA,* 87 (1972), 53–63

Rejects the dominant readings of the novel that either emphasize the tragic consequences of repression or the repression of desires as "stages" in Maggie's spiritual development. Rather, Maggie's defeat results from her legitimate desires and her equally legitimate bonds to family, which demand renunciation of her desires.

262   Ermarth, Elizabeth
"Maggie Tulliver's Long Suicide", *Studies in English Literature,* 14 (1974), 587–601

The social norms that "exert a heavy influence" on Maggie are sexist; being female is a key to her tragedy. While GE is sympathetic to women's need to accept those norms, she sees acquiescence in them as in effect suicide. Maggie's return is the "strongest possible argument . . . for doing the opposite", as GE herself did in going off to London and then living with Lewes.

263   Swann, Brian
"The Mill on the Floss and the Form of Tragedy", *English Miscellany,* 24 (1974), 199–232

A detailed examination of the structure of tragedy in the novel, which, Swann argues, is based on a series of Aristotelean reversals. Swann discusses various aspects of GE's theory of tragedy as formulated in her essays, and argues that tragedy in *The Mill on the Floss* differs in kind from tragedy in the earlier novels.

264   Auerbach, Nina
"The Power of Hunger: Demonism and Maggie Tulliver",
Nineteenth-Century Fiction, 30 (1975), 150–71

The Mill on the Floss opposes provincial respectability to
emotional explosiveness, and there are many suggestions of
demonism associated with Maggie. The demonic connotations
of unruly hair, Maggie's fetishistic doll, her emotional volatility,
her penchant for death, her alliance with trees and animals — all
of these are expressed in the novel's "subterranean language" of
Gothic romance.

(FEMINISM)

265   Putzell, Sara M.
"'An Antagonism of Valid Claims': The Dynamics of *The Mill
on the Floss*", *Studies in the Novel,* 7 (1975), 227–44

Another treatment of the ending of the novel, considering
whether the death is "a translation or an escape". The narrative
and Maggie are described as being full of antitheses. The ending
is an attempt to sustain the irreconcilable antagonisms
(especially between self-denial and self-fulfilment) in the same
act.

266   New, Peter
"Moral Tradition in *The Mill on the Floss*", *English,* 27 (1978),
133–47

GE is opposed to the doctrine of consequences, and instead
insists on developing the moral habit of choosing reasonably.

267   Arac, Jonathan
"Rhetoric and Realism in Nineteenth-Century Fiction:
Hyperbole in *The Mill on the Floss*", *ELH,* 46 (1979), 673–92

Uses the novel to demonstrate that idea of the nineteenth-century
novel as manifesting a naive faith in its powers of representation
is misguided. Finds in the novel two "incommensurable"
patterns, "realistic" harmony and completeness as opposed to
"romantic" excess and disruption. "Eliot's awareness of this
conflict makes her book an active clash between the hope of a
fitting language and the recognition that language is never at one
with reality".

268   Jacobus, Mary
        "The Question of Language: Men of Maxims and *The Mill on
        the Floss*", *Critical Inquiry,* 8 (1981), 207–22

        Working with Irigaray's formulation, Jacobus seeks a text that
        will allow "putting the question of our social organization of
        gender". She takes the opening chapter of Part Two, which
        presents an anti-feminist pedagogy and "raises
        questions . . . about the functioning of both sexual ideology
        and language". The disruption of the formulas of the dominant
        culture is a function both of the woman writer and of Maggie
        herself. "*The Mill on the Floss* uncovers the divide between the
        language of maxims of the dominant culture and language itself
        which undoes them".

                                                            (FEMINISM)

269   Wasserman, Renata R. Mantner
        "Narrative Logic and the Form of Tradition in *The Mill on the
        Floss*", *Studies in the Novel,* 14 (1982), 266–79

        Another consideration of the endlessly provoking question of
        the novel's ending, beginning with a useful summary of what
        others have thought the problem to be (but not completely
        consonant with the very extensive literature on the subject).
        Wasserman suggests that the death of the heroine "destabilizes
        the Victorian convention that the 'dark', passionate woman
        must die" because unlike other such heroines, Maggie dies not
        from "moral and natural necessity" but from a kind of accident,
        unrelated to moral culpability.

270   Kucich, John
        "George Eliot and Objects: Meaning as Matter in *The Mill on
        the Floss*", *Dickens Studies Annual,* 12 (1983), 319–40

        In GE the "conjunction of man and matter always reveals the
        impoverished, reductive character of human efforts to
        appropriate the world". There are no "purely natural" objects
        in *The Mill on the Floss* — all infused with the taint of commerce.
        Kucich wants to show that GE's use of the human as the standard
        of value for objects is contradicted by her unease at the way no
        objects are natural, all are made to subserve human interests.
        "GE's humanism . . . is severely tested by her reaction against
        the scientific and industrial pragmatism of her age, which helped
        to make all human designs on the world appear to be rapacious".

271 Fleishman, Avrom
FIGURES OF AUTOBIOGRAPHY: THE LANGUAGE OF
SELF-WRITING (Berkeley: University of California Press,
1983), pp. 235–56

The Mill on the Floss is not only "a characteristic Victorian
autobiographical novel but marks a crucial turning point in the
use of traditional forms and figures in fictional self-
conception". It rejects "the biblical figures of traditional
autobiography, with their burden of typological promise and
divine underwriting of a life". The novel implicitly criticizes "the
entire canon of autobiographical writing". The plot is
correlative to her personal experience, working out her tragic
sense of modern life. Realistic commitment compromises the
traditions, as e.g. the edenic start is not edenic. In rewriting the
spiritual autobiography tradition, she adapts the modern
Bildungsroman, and "allows authorial consciousness to absorb
and embrace the entire text".

Silas Marner

(See also Haddakin in 47)

272   Thale, Jerome
"George Eliot's Fable for Her Time", *College English,* 19, (1958), 141–6

The two halves of the story are generically different (realism and pastoral). Silas's is a kind of allegory of modern England, moving through the same kind of intellectual and religious crisis that GE did. The two halves play off against each other, offering alternative readings of the modern world.

273   Thomson, Fred C.
"The Theme of Alienation in *Silas Marner*", *Nineteenth-Century Fiction,* 20 (1965), 69–84

Argues that the novel belongs to the mainstream of GE's novels and represents an important development in her vision of tragic life. Discusses the double plot and alienated characters, features that make up the tragic element of the later novels, notably *Middlemarch.*

274   Milner, Ian
"Structure and Quality in Silas Marner", *Studies in English Literature,* 6 (1966), 717–29

Milner defends the novel as morally serious and artistically admirable, challenging the tendency to see the novel as "charming" (Leavis) or as a pleasant pastoral, and supports his defence with an examination of the novel's structure and two-fold theme: man's inhumanity to man and the conflict of moral values and social classes.

275   Carroll, David R.
"*Silas Marner:* Reversing the Oracles of Religion", *Literary Monographs,* 1 (1967), 167–200; 312–14

In a complex and impressive argument, Carroll shows how the two stories — of Godfrey and of Silas — are expressions of the same theme. Both of these central figures degenerate through most of the novel. Each is redeemed through action, and they finally confront each other near the conclusion.

276   Swann, Brian
        "*Silas Marner* and the New Mythus", *Criticism,* 18 (1976), 101–21

Silas Marner is a novel in which realism is made to include "subliminal patterns of regeneration, fairy tale, and myth". Its subject is mythic creation and regeneration. Swann examines the way the novel's "new mythus" consists of change and creation, and focuses on images of light that embody the miraculous.

277   Dessner, Lawrence Jay
        "The Autobiographical Matrix of *Silas Marner*", *Studies in the Novel,* 11 (1979), 251–82

Argues for a complex relationship betwen the situations and emotional patterns in GE's life and their counterparts in *Silas Marner*. Using biographical information, particularly from the letters, Dessner focuses on the period just before the composition of the novel, a time of isolation, depression and poor health.

278   Simpson, Peter
        "Crisis and Recovery: William Wordsworth, George Eliot, and *Silas Marner*", *University of Toronto Quarterly,* 48 (1979), 95–114

The novel synthesizes the "social truth of the lyrical ballads with the deep psychological truth of *The Prelude*". It is "displaced autobiography" that re-enacts the pattern of crisis and recovery, the central events of GE's and Wordsworth's lives. The novel is a study of the growth of the artist's mind, and it dramatizes the "process of its own conception and gestation".

279   Hawes, Donald
        "Chance in *Silas Marner*", *English,* 31 (1982), 213–18

Locates a point in GE where lack of dramatic power is manifest — the comment on Favourable Chance in *Silas Marner*. GE evades the implications of lot-drawing in Lantern Yard, and the plot suggests the virtues of chance despite the narrator's explicit denunciation of it. Godfrey is condemned for relying on chance, but Silas is not, while Dolly's trust in Providence can be interpreted as a trust in chance. Hawes argues that the inconsistency results from GE's shift in method, which makes the novel a legendary tale.

280   McLaverty, James
"Comtean Fetishism in *Silas Marner*", *Nineteenth-Century Fiction,* 36 (1982), 318–36

Fetishism for Comte is the first stage of man's progress, and it helps explain the distinction between Silas, who "spontaneously adopts a child", and Godfrey, who denies his own. Fetishism for Comte develops at the stage of human history when men are most dependent on their feelings. To supplement David Carroll's reading, McLaverty offers "an account of how Comte's system provides the vital link between the myths of the community and its domestic life and slow progress towards civilization".

(PHILOSOPHY)

281   Cohen, Susan R.
"A History and a Metamorphosis: Continuity and Discontinuity in *Silas Marner*", *Texas Studies in Literature and Language,* 25 (1983), 410–26

Argues that *Silas Marner* clearly illustrates "the nightmare of disintegration and discontinuity" that GE suffered in her own break from Christianity and to which she subjects all her heroines. "Continuities and connections are both necessary and fictitious", GE suggests, and Cohen finds this point dramatized in the Rainbow tavern scene. The novel does not confirm Dolly Winthrop's providential faith and disrupts its own orderly sequence, while law and chance "compete for moral allegiance" in the narrative.

Romola

(See also Levine in 47; and Gezari in 50)

282　Robinson, Carole
"*Romola:* A Reading of the Novel", *Victorian Studies,* 6 (1962), 29–42

A convincing argument about the novel's achievements and failures, focusing on the conflicts of Romola. She faces the most difficult choices and can easily be identified with the Victorian intellectual. In fact, *Romola's* determination to make labour compensate for loss of faith and spiritual values is modern, not medieval, and the novel's failures result from GE's "uncertain faith in the affirmations she proposes".

283　DeLaura, David
"*Romola* and the Origin of the Paterian View of Life", *Nineteenth-Century Fiction,* 21 (1966), 225–33

Maintains that Pater's reading of *Romola* "may well have been the impetus that set [him] on the road to the essay in *Studies in the History of the Renaissance*", and locates the strongest evidence for his argument in the repeated sympathetically described appearances of Savonarola. Thematic and structural parallels between *Romola* and *Marius the Epicurean* provide evidence of influence.

284　Poston, III, Lawrence
"Setting and Theme in *Romola*", *Nineteenth-Century Fiction,* 20 (1966), 355–66

A discussion of the importance of the historical setting and of the network of relationships between the individual and the state in his defence of the novel as a "historical romance".

285　Hill, Donald L.
"Pater's Debt to *Romola*", *Nineteenth-Century Fiction,* 22 (1968), 361–77

A refutation of DeLaura's claim in 283. Examines Pater's remarks and GE's fiction and her references to Savonarola. He concludes that they provide no evidence of an influence of *Romola* in Pater's *The Renaissance* and that it is just as likely that Pater read other material which suggested the same techniques and themes.

(COMPARISON)

286   Fleishman, Avrom
THE ENGLISH HISTORICAL NOVEL: WALTER SCOTT TO VIRGINIA WOOLF (Baltimore: Johns Hopkins University Press, 1971), pp. 155–63

Romola dramatizes the duality of the Renaissance — its individualism and its inherited tradition of piety. The novel embodies GE's Comtean concept of historical development. Fleishman concludes that although GE failed to animate the historical background, she successfully created "a severely conscientious portrait of a total society".

287   Bullen, J.B.
"George Eliot's *Romola* as a Positivist Allegory", *Review of English Studies,* 26 (1975), 425–35

Written in the form of a historical novel, *Romola* contains an allegorical account of the development of man's moral consciousness that suggests Comte's account of man's moral and intellectual evolution. Bullen traces some of the connections and provides an overview of Comte's positivism.

(PHILOSOPHY)

288   Bonaparte, Felicia
THE TRIPTYCH AND THE CROSS: THE CENTRAL MYTHS OF GEORGE ELIOT'S POETIC IMAGINATION (New York: New York University Press, 1979)

An extensive study of the complex and elaborate mythological structure of *Romola,* which Bonaparte claims as the "first mythological novel in English". Bonaparte examines in minute detail the significance of the novel's mythological allusions and their relationship to its epic and poetic form. She considers also what she regards as the novel's exploration, through mythology, of the growth of Western civilization and the cultural conflicts among the Greek, Roman and Christian worlds.

289   Anderson, R.F.
        "George Eliot and the Publication of *Romola*", *Publishing History,* 8 (1982), 5–39

A careful history of the Blackwoods' relation to *Romola,* suggesting that GE's decision to switch to Smith, Elder was not quite such a surprise as has been said. Despite the Blackwoods' friendship with her, GE felt that Blackwood undervalued her literary worth. She rejected Blackwood's offer of £3000 for copyright on her first four books. In this careful step-by-step record of the negotiations between Lewes (for GE) and Blackwood, and Lewes and Smith, Elder, GE does not emerge admirably. John Blackwood emerges as the most honourable, and perhaps the shrewdest of the figures in this slightly shabby literary episode.

290   Witemeyer, Hugh
        "George Eliot's *Romola* and Bulwer Lytton's *Rienzi*", *Studies in the Novel* (Spring 1983), 62–71

Argues that Bonaparte is wrong is discounting the influence of *Rienzi* on *Romola.* "Bulwer's theory and practice of historical romance helped GE define the aims and to organize the narrative of her first extended effort in that genre". Bulwer's theory that historical romance should be externally empirical and factual and that it should explain fact with the internal history of the characters (where the romance lies) is important to GE. GE seems to adopt Bulwer's view that the internal can be discovered by *analogy.*

Felix Holt

(See also Gallagher and Butwin in 49; Kettle in 47; 159, Robbins)

291   Wright, Walter F.
"George Eliot as Industrial Reformer", *PMLA,* 56 (1941),
1107–15

Details the philosophical background of GE's approach to social
questions, arguing that she "was trying to fit economic and
social progress into a cosmic pattern . . . evolutionary, yet
directed".

292   Williams, Raymond
"Felix Holt", CULTURE AND SOCIETY: 1780–1950 (New
York: Columbia University Press, 1958; New York: Doubleday
Anchor, 1960), pp. 110–18

Distinguishes the quality of GE's novel as opposed to other
industrial novels, despite the fact that it has much in common
with them. GE's handling of the personal themes and of Felix's
preaching (a front for GE) is characteristic of the period and very
weak. Her position from behind the façade is "of a Carlyle
without the energy". What distinguishes GE is her sense of
society as a complicated inheritance. But GE's sense of
complication keeps her from being able to conceive of valuable
social action at all. "It is indeed a mark of a deadlock in society
when so fine an intelligence and so quick a sympathy can
conceive no more than this".

293   Thomson, Fred C.
"The Genesis of *Felix Holt*", *PMLA,* 74 (1959), 576–84

Drawing largely upon external evidence (GE's and Lewes's
letters, journals and reading), Thomson argues that the adultery
of Mrs Transome and Jermyn was the genesis of the novel.
Politics and the role of Felix "were probably afterthoughts",
brought into the foreground later in the composition.

294   Thomson, Fred C.
"Felix Holt as Classic Tragedy", *Nineteenth-Century Fiction,*
16 (1961), 47–58

The political material was not part of GE's original design. Her interest in tragedy developed at this time, and the Transome story qualifies as tragedy in terms of her own definition. GE was adhering to the principles set forth in "Notes on the Spanish Gipsy and Tragedy in General". Thomson believes that GE fell short of her aim, but "as an experiment in expanding the horizons of prose fiction, *Felix Holt* deserves more commendation that it has received".

295   Carroll, David R.
       "*Felix Holt:* Society as Protagonist", *Nineteenth-Century Fiction,* 17 (1962), 237–52

Felix Holt begins to take up the concern of the last three novels, confronted first in *Romola:* the breakdown of the metaphor of the social organism. Felix must learn that his role as reformer of Esther Lyon is integral to his role as reformer of the working class. His character is thus not static, but participates in GE's discovery that no attempt to reform society can succeed without a recognition of the importance of the individual.

296   Thomson, Fred C.
       "The Legal Plot in *Felix Holt*", *Studies in English Literature,* 7 (1967), 691–704

Although GE's treatment of the law is not entirely successful, the legal technicalities are related to the novel's central theme — heredity and "slowly accruing Nemesis". Focuses on Frederic Harrison's detailed legal advice solicited by GE during composition of the novel.

297   Levine, George
       "Introduction", FELIX HOLT, THE RADICAL (New York: W.W. Norton, 1970)

The "radicalism" of the novel is conservative, based on an encompassing vision of organic interconnection of all things. That vision, tested against the power of real events, leads to a denial of the possibility of radical change. Felix, in his political and moral insistence, is subject to the power of events. Esther is the real hero, developing a power of vision that allows her to see connections hitherto invisible to her. The novel affirms traditional moral values against political change.

298   Thomson, Fred C.
"Politics and Society in *Felix Holt*", THE CLASSIC BRITISH
NOVEL, ed. Howard Harper and Charles Edge (Athens,
Georgia: University of Georgia Press, 1972), pp. 103–20

Traces GE's somewhat conservative political views in *Felix Holt,*
arguing that her mind characteristically transmuted the age's
specific political currents into broad humanitarian concepts.

299   Bamber, Linda
"Self-Defeating Politics in George Eliot's *Felix Holt*", *Victorian
Studies,* 18 (1975), 419–35

GE, as a political novelist, dramatizes "the antagonism of valid
claims" and the contest between private and public morality. She
denies unequivocal validity to either side of conflict, and
recommends "sympathy and respect for the representatives of
entrenched interests and resistance to a vulgar indentification
with the champions of reform". Her instinctive commitment to
see the other side has drawbacks in politics but is central to her art
and morality. Great as a political novelist of the Creons, she is
weak with her Antigones — Deronda, Ladislaw, Felix Holt.
GE's commitment to personal morality and to the individual
leads her to a conservative political position with which "she is
extremely uneasy". Change can only come by unifying private
and public interest, and GE is really committed to a tragic vision
of conflict which she tries to avert.

300   Swann, Charles
"Evolution and Revolution: Politics and Form in *Felix Holt* and
The Revolution in Tanner's Lane", LITERATURE,
SOCIETY, AND THE SOCIOLOGY OF LITERATURE, ed.
John Coombes, Peter Hulme, David Musselwhite and Richard
Osborne (Colchester: University of Essex, 1977).

Takes "Mark Rutherford's" novel as a deliberate criticism "of
the views of history, politics and literary form embodied in *Felix
Holt*". Rutherford can allow for radical change, while GE
cannot. Her conception of history is less alert to process and
change and *Felix Holt* evades history in its turn to domestic
drama. The analysis of Rutherford's novel shows its alternatives
to GE and a more complicated sense of history.

                                              (COMPARISON)

301   Zimmerman, Bonnie
        "*Felix Holt* and the True Power of Womanhood", *English Literary History,* 46 (1979), 432–51

The novel is concerned not only with male politics but with the "problem of woman's true power". GE's sexual politics "are rooted . . . in the differences between the sexes", and she accepted the ideology that women's power depends on "submission to oppression". In *Felix Holt* GE connects the Reform Movement with sexual politics, and it gives form to her strong ambivalence on the subject. It demonstrates the oppressive narrowness of women's lives but cannot support the political means currently being suggested for their enfranchisement and freedom.

(FEMINISM)

302   Sheets, Robin
        "*Felix Holt:* Language, the Bible, and the Problematic of Meaning", *Nineteenth-Century Fiction,* 37 (1982), 146–69

Discusses the novel in terms of the community constructed from language. In the novel it is a Babel, without trust, where language obscures and is ineffectual. Interpretation becomes arbitrary. The issue of community through language is related to GE's "own anxieties about authorship". The concern for how people read and speak helps explain "the significance of many minor characters and incidents", and to unify the two strains of narrative. GE tries to face the question of the purpose of her own text if a community cannot determine its purpose, and to consider how it is possible for her as novelist to fulfil her responsibilities.

Middlemarch

(See also 257; Armstrong in 47; Gordan, Levine and Meikle in 50)

303 James, Henry
     Review of *Middlemarch, Galaxy,* 15 (1873), 424–28

Criticizes the formal expansiveness of the novel: "as GE's mind is preeminently contemplative and analytic, nothing is more natural than that her manner should be discursive and expansive". Despite lack of concentration, the novel has remarkable elements — the character of Dorothea, in particular. But the story inadequately develops her and the more interesting material is often displaced by the trivial. Deeply appreciative of GE's qualities of mind and of the maturity of her creation of her "little World", James yet concludes that *Middlemarch* "sets a limit . . . to the development of the old-fashioned English novel".

304 Kettle, Arnold
     "George Eliot: *Middlemarch*", AN INTRODUCTION TO THE ENGLISH NOVEL: FROM DEFOE TO GEORGE ELIOT (London: Hutchinson, 1951), vol. 1, pp. 171–90

Middlemarch makes no advance in art over Jane Austen, but merely extends her methods. GE's language in heavier both in emotional freight and in moral generalization. She works in placing characters within a social medium, but there is a contrast between "the success of the parts and failure of the whole". The novel lacks "that final vibrant intensity of the living organism". Its view of society is "static", and the various parts do not really interpenetrate or grow from each other. Society is imagined as a determining force, not something living in interaction with individual people. GE's thought is mechanistic and undialectic, and this forces her into idealism. Nevertheless, her attempt "to convey the inter-relatedness of life" was important and original.

305 Steiner, F. George
     "A Preface to *Middlemarch*", *Nineteenth-Century Fiction,* 9 (1955), 262–79

Views the novel in the light of the great continental tradition and finds it wanting both in structure and in the quality of the authorial voice. The failure is in narrative technique, characteristic of nineteenth-century English fiction, which "places a screen of avoidance between author and page".

306   Beaty, Jerome
        "History by Indirection: The Era of Reform in *Middlemarch*", *Victorian Studies,* 1 (1957), 173–9

Demonstrates how GE integrates history into her narrative inconspicuously, carefully setting events within the context of large historical developments, punctuating and paralleling the characters' activities, and making their implication in history richly important to our understanding.

307   Anderson, Quentin
        "George Eliot in *Middlemarch*", FROM DICKENS TO HARDY, ed. Boris Ford (Baltimore: Penguin Books, 1958)

An influential reading of the novel, one of the first to see it as dominated by the image of "the web".

308   Beaty, Jerome
        "The Forgotten Past of Will Ladislaw", *Nineteenth-Century Fiction,* 13 (1958), 159–63

Suggests the possibility, with strong evidence, that Will Ladislaw may have been Jewish, preparing the way, for GE, for the full-scale treatment of Jewish questions in *Daniel Deronda.*

309   Carroll, David
        "Unity Through Analogy: An Interpretation of *Middlemarch*", *Victorian Studies,* 2 (1959), 305–16

The richness of the Victorian novel can be exemplified in "'the undertones of thought' in *Middlemarch*". These lead to "a realization" that the novel achieves "unity through analogy". The relations among the blocs of characters are determined by an attempt, like Dorothea's, "to find a principle that will unify the fragmentariness which [the] structure of the novel postulates". The unifying principle is to be found in "one's relations to one's fellow human beings". Everyone in the novel has to work out a personal cosmology (on analogy with Dorothea's), and the theme extends out into society and politics.

310   Beaty, Jerome
       MIDDLEMARCH: FROM NOTEBOOK TO NOVEL: A
       STUDY OF GEORGE ELIOT'S CREATIVE METHOD
       (Urbana: University of Illinois Press, 1960)

The major, definitive study of the development of the novel from
GE's first ideas about "Miss Brooke". The book combines
literary acumen with some excellent detective work determining
the points at which the two stories were joined. Beaty's analysis
of the interview between Dorothea and Rosamond, which he
claims GE pointed towards as the dramatic climax of the novel, is
excellent, and provides several of many important critical
insights into the novel derived from an understanding of its
development and structure.

311   Stallknecht, Newton P.
       "Resolution and Independence: A Reading of *Middlemarch*",
       TWELVE ORIGINAL ESSAYS ON GREAT ENGLISH
       NOVELS, ed. Charles Shapiro (Detroit: Wayne State University
       Press, 1960), pp. 125–52

A somewhat rudimentary discussion that defends the
"resolution and independence" of Dorothea's decision to marry
Will, as well as the novel's didactic, analytic, intellectual tone,
against the complaint of critics like Leslie Stephen and F.R.
Leavis.

312   Hagan, John
       "*Middlemarch:* Narrative Unity in the Story of Dorothea
       Brooke", *Nineteenth-Century Fiction,* 16 (1961), 17–32

The story of Dorothea is examined to show that it is the
construction of "a highly conscious craftsman". Hagan traces
the *Bildungsroman* form through illusion, awareness, purgation
and the replacement of misconceptions with "more adequate
substitutes".

313   Daiches, David
       GEORGE ELIOT: *MIDDLEMARCH* (London: Edward
       Arnold; Great Neck, N.Y.: Baron's Educational Series, 1963)

An introduction designed for the college student, but Daiches'
new critical method excludes biographical material. The book
closely examines the novel's handling of time, narrative,
characterization and theme.

314   Hardy, Barabara
        "Implication and Incompleteness: George Eliot's
        Middlemarch", THE APPROPRIATE FORM: AN ESSAY
        ON THE NOVEL (London: Athlone Press, 1964), pp. 105–31

Consideration of the formal qualities of the novel, emphasizing
that "the form is the means to the ends of good story, moral
argument, and the imitation of life". The essay shows how the
novel is "only restrictedly truthful in its treatment of sexuality".
Casaubon's impotence is crucial to the narrative, and is
successfully intimated. The real weakness of the novel, both
formal and thematic, is the balancing treatment (or its absence)
of sexuality in Will Ladislaw. The "poetic unity" of the novel
does not suffice to produce "completeness" of treatment.
Dorothea's sexual innocence with Ladislaw suggests GE's
complicity in her lack of self-knowledge, very uncharacteristic of
the rest of the novel and the Casaubon sequences.

315   Hardy, Barbara
        MIDDLEMARCH: CRITICAL APPROACHES TO THE
        NOVEL (New York: Oxford University Press, 1967)

Eight generally strong essays: Mark Schorer, "The Structure of
the Novel"; W.J. Harvey, "The Intellectual Background of the
Novel"; Jerome Beaty, "The Text of the Novel"; Derek
Oldfield, "The Language of the Novel"; Hilda M. Hulme, "The
Language of the Novel: Imagery"; W.J. Harvey, "Criticism of
the Novel"; Barbara Hardy, "The Surface of the Novel";
J.M.S. Tompkins, "A Plea for Ancient Lights".

316   Hulme, Hilda
        "*Middlemarch* as Science Fiction: Notes on Language and
        Imagery", *Novel,* 2 (1968), 36–45

317   Feltes, N.N.
        "George Eliot's 'Pier-Glass': The Development of a
        Metaphor", *Modern Philology,* 67 (1969), 69–71

The "eminent philosopher" is Herbert Spencer, who had talked
to GE about the phenomenon, and took the metaphor as a way
of describing the obstruction to scientific objectivity. Compares
the use of the metaphor to that of Ruskin and Spencer.

318   Knoepflmacher, U.C.
"*Middlemarch:* Affirmation through Compromise'',
LAUGHTER AND DESPAIR: READINGS IN TEN
NOVELS OF THE VICTORIAN ERA (Berkeley: University of
California Press, 1971), pp. 168–201 (109–35)

In *Middlemarch* GE attempts to build "a construct against
despair through which she could preserve Maggie's idealism
amidst a prosaic world''. Knoepflmacher shows how the novel
exposes and punishes illusions, like Thackeray's *Vanity Fair,* but
how it diverges in plotting the complex convergence of her
characters' fates. The narrator connects the strands of story and
complicates by forcing alternative points of view. Deeply
concerned with connections, the novel concludes with a balanced
expression of the novelist's "mixture of hope and despondency,
acceptance and revulsion''. (Chapter 4, dealing with *The Mill on
the Floss* and *The Ordeal of Richard Feverel,* examines how each
novel begins in a comic vein but ends in a tragic catastrophe
which reveals the impossibility of social integration and
resolution and the irreconcilable gap between past and present.)
(COMPARISON)

319   Mason, Michael York
"*Middlemarch* and History'', *Nineteenth-Century Fiction,* 25
(1971), 417–31

Traces the relation between the period of the First Reform Bill
depicted in the novel and the period in which GE wrote the novel,
especially the sense of political crisis.

320   Mason, Michael York
"*Middlemarch* and Science: Problems of Life and Mind'',
Review of English Studies, 22 (1971), 151–69

Examines the importance of science to the novel, and shows the
connection of GE's "realism" to science (distinguishing it from
Ruskin's). Considers Lewes's *Problems of Life and Mind* in
relation to GE's notions of objectivity and the creative
imagination. In discussing *Middlemarch,* Mason shows how GE
uses Lewes and evolutionary biology to imply a view of the world
that allows both for spontaneous ideas and for "an outer world
to which those ideas will correspond''.
(SCIENCE)

321   Swann, Brian
        "*Middlemarch:* Realism and Symbolic Form", *English Literary History,* 39 (1972), 279–308

Henry James's criticism of GE's art raises an important problem: there was no critical language to deal with her aesthetic experiments — the dominant idea of "organic unity". GE, no mere literalist, extends the meaning of historical realism "by embodying the 'mythopoeic aspect of history'". GE adopts a symbolic form, what she thought of as the "higher form of art", and in *Middlemarch* creates a new form, "symbolic realism", where everything is related to everything else without sacrificing its particularity. Swann goes on to discuss various aspects and elements of this form with detailed analysis of the novel.

322   Scott, James F.
        "George Eliot, Positivism, and the Social Vision of *Middlemarch*", *Victorian Studies,* 16 (1972), 59–76

Scott argues that GE's "complex attitude towards Positivism figures importantly in the structure and character analysis of *Middlemarch*". After tracing briefly GE's reading of Comte, Scott discusses letters Eliot exchanged with Frederic Harrison, who asked GE to treat problems that are central to *Middlemarch*. Scott analyses GE's complex relation to Comte and Harrison's thought, noting how that relation is expressed in the details of *Middlemarch*.

                                                    (PHILOSOPHY)

323   Coles, Robert
        "Irony in the Mind's Life-Maturity: George Eliot's *Middlemarch*", *Virginia Quarterly Review,* 49 (1973), 526–52

Observing that *Middlemarch* presents no central argument, Coles himself presents not so much a criticial argument as a meditation on the novel's theme of life's "indefiniteness". Coles discusses the ways in which GE compels us to regard "moral ambiguities and complexities of character and temperament with increasing relativity".

324   Ellmann, Richard
        "Dorothea's Husbands: Some Biographical Speculations",

GOLDEN CODGERS: BIOGRAPHICAL SPECULATIONS
(New York: Oxford University Press, 1973), pp. 17–38

Speculations on the originals for Casaubon, concluding that
whatever men might fit (Spencer? Brabant? Pattison?),
Casaubon is "the repository of GE's inferior qualities".
Ladislaw, usually associated with Lewes, may well be her
ultimate husband, the young Johnnie Cross. Interesting
evidence is supplied.

(BIOGRAPHIES)

325   Swann, Brian
"*Middlemarch* and Myth", *Nineteenth-Century Fiction,* 28
(1973), 210–14

Brief discussion of GE's use of the classical myth of the rape of
Persephone in *Middlemarch.* Although GE's use of the myth is
"self-conscious and by way of extended analogy . . . it takes its
part in the complicated symbolic structure, for it is based on the
symbolic values of light and dark".

326   Adam, Ian
THIS PARTICULAR WEB (Toronto: University of Toronto
Press, 1975)

Five original essays originally delivered at a *Middlemarch*
centenary conference at Calgary. The paper by David Carroll,
"*Middlemarch* and the Externality of Fact", is a classic analysis
of GE's conception of knowledge as it manifests itself in
narrative form. The general level of quality of the collection is
very high. Barbara Hardy, "*Middlemarch* and the Passions";
Gordon S. Haight, "George Eliot's 'Eminent Failure', Will
Ladislaw"; U.C. Knoepflmacher, "Fusing Fact and Myth: the
New Reality of *Middlemarch*"; Gillian Beer, "Myth and the
Single Consciousness: *Middlemarch* and 'The Lifted Veil'".

327   Greenberg, Robert A.
"Plexuses and Ganglia: Some Scientific Allusions in
Middlemarch", *Nineteenth-Century Fiction,* 30 (1975), 33–52

Insisting that none of the novel's demanding scientific allusions
is irrelevant to the novel's design, Greenberg draws upon the
"Quarry" for *Middlemarch,* Lewes's scientific writing, and a

great deal of scientific background material to elucidate the meaning and relevance of scientific allusions in the novel.

(SCIENCE)

328   Kiely, Robert
"The Limits of Dialogue in *Middlemarch*", THE WORLDS OF VICTORIAN FICTION, ed. J.H. Buckley (Cambridge, Mass.: Harvard University Press, 1975), pp. 103–23

The essay does not deal centrally with *Middlemarch*. Language is crucial to GE, who is rigorously correct in usage, but in *Adam Bede* she validates her character's rich colloquial idiom. "The object of the word is communication". The essay examines several novels in the light of this objective and the obstacles people and society place in the way.

329   Knoepflmacher, U.C.
"Middlemarch: An Avuncular View", *Nineteenth-Century Fiction,* 30 (1975), 53–81

The uncle figures in the novel demonstrate the absence of a sacramental universe such as is implied in the "Prelude". They "pervert the traditional role of father substitute, provider, and agent for justice assigned to the uncle or *avunculus* in an ordered universe". Mr Brooke is singled out as object for irony despite his benevolent intentions. He is responsible for Dorothea's plight. As opposed to the enfeebled imagination and dabbling intelligence of Brooke, there is the genuine avuncular figure of the narrator, who can integrate and connect.

330   Miller, J. Hillis
"Optic and Semiotic in *Middlemarch*", THE WORLDS OF VICTORIAN FICTION, ed. J.H. Buckley (Cambridge, Mass.: Harvard University Press, 1975), pp. 125–45

GE intends a totalized vision of society and the world, and the medium of this totalization is specificity combined with generalization. Miller argues that the metaphors used in the novel to register interrelations through time are in fact contradictory and disrupt the effort at totalization. "The metaphor of the complex moving web . . . is . . . contradicted by the metaphor of vision". This essay is closely related to 122.

331   Blake, Kathleen
"*Middlemarch* and the Woman Question", *Nineteenth-Century Fiction,* 31 (1976), 285–312

Considers various arguments against feminist approaches to the novel. Blake argues that the "Finale's" indictment of society for Dorothea's fate is sustained by the rest of the novel. Considers the theme of vocation in relation to women's condition and argues that GE does not leave the novel with depressing conclusions for women but opens up possibilities within the historical constraints she records. This essay provides in the process of its analysis useful surveys of feminist opinion on GE to date.

(FEMINISM)

332   Hardy, Barbara
"*Middlemarch:* Public and Private Worlds", *English,* 25 (1976), 5–26

Middlemarch offers the first analysis of historical consciousness, an analysis that involves recognition that private experience shapes the sense of the public, just as the public life shapes the private world. GE locates the link between public and private in individual consciousness.

333   Roazen, Deborah
"*Middlemarch* and the Wordsworthian Imagination", *English Studies,* 58 (1977), 411–25

Although not generally considered Wordsworthian in the way of the earlier novels, *Middlemarch* reveals GE's aesthetic and moral kinship with Wordsworth in "its affirmation of the value to be found in ordinary experience" and the crucial notes of memory and the continuity of experience.

334   Hertz, Neil
"Recognizing Casaubon", *Glyph,* 6 (1979), 24–41
Elaborates the readings of Hillis Miller in 123 and 330. Characters in GE are both interpreters and texts available for interpretation, and GE both affirms a traditional sense of character and offers figures who are merely clusters of signs. Hertz exposes contradictions in GE's treatment of recipients of moral generosity, like Casaubon, who, as a figure for writing in

the novel, as an object of generosity, and as narcissist, puts to the question "the validity of the novelist's imagination of others".

335   Ginsburg, Michael Peled
        "Pseudonym, Epigraphs, and Narrative Voice: *Middlemarch* the Problem of Authorship", *English Literary History*, 47 (1980), 542–58

Considers the "split of the text against itself", its strategy of shifting point of view that at once assures the emergence of truth and questions and negates its own enterprise. Ginsburg parallels the problematic status of author as origin of text (as evinced here in pseudonym and epigraph), and the question of the status of a subject as an origin of an utterance.

336   Bonaparte, Felicia
        "*Middlemarch:* The Genesis of Myth in the English Novel: The Relationship Between Literary Form and the Modern Predicament", *Notre Dame English Journal*, 8 (1981), 107–54

An ambitious essay taking *Middlemarch* as the first symbolic novel in English. Its realistic narrative is indicted by its symbolic structure. In *Middlemarch* GE tries to write "a history of the world". Bonaparte studies the symbols in considering the large question of whether it is possible to lead a grand life here or whether history is merely circular. Mythology, freed from "its theological prison", gives the modern world a gift of faith. GE rejects both the solutions of science and those of a strict allegorical reading (held in the Middle Ages to reveal in history a theological truth). The synthesis comes with Ladislaw, the "mythological figure of Dionysus". Bonaparte's reading tries to demonstrate that the empiricism that made realism possible made the symbolic novel necessary, and she provides her key to all *Middlemarch* mythologies in her quest to restore with GE the lost legacy of romance.

337   Miller, D.A.
        NARRATIVE AND ITS DISCONTENTS: PROBLEMS OF CLOSURE IN THE TRADITIONAL NOVEL (Princeton: Princeton University Press, 1981)

The novels point towards a condition that transcends the impermanence, mixed conditions and moral difficulties of the narratable world. But they cannot achieve the transcendence they seek because for Eliot the narratable is the true, the transcendent is the dream. Process does not stop. Miller reads *Middlemarch* with remarkably sharp attention to detail, and demonstrates movingly that within the terms of the realist mode, GE will not falsify, and thus she will not commit herself to the possibilities she seeks to assert or discover. An impatience with the narratable, which inevitably means a frustration of transcendence, marks some of GE's struggle, and Miller throws her career in a fresh light as he relocates both her frustration and her narrative honesty by brilliant readings of *Middlemarch*.

338   Marotta, Kenny
         "*Middlemarch:* the 'Home Epic'", *Genre,* 15 (1982), 403–20

GE's disclaimers of epic intention reveal her "persistent consciousness of the world of epic action". Points to a contradiction in the novel — "praise of the heroism of surrender of ambition". The focus on epic ambition is obscured by the "novelistic polemic against romance". With no outlet for action, renunciation is the only outlet for conscious ambition, and the would-be hero becomes a critic of unworthy action. Marriage becomes the test of epic worthiness. It is by an epic standard that GE's characters are to be judged.

339   Wiesenfarth, Joseph
         "*Middlemarch:* The Language of Art", *PMLA,* 97 (1982), 363–77

Wiesenfarth seeks to discuss "the theory of art that composes the novel . . . . For *Middlemarch* contains its own aesthetic theory, thus providing a context in which we can interpret the novel as a whole and understand its many references to the arts". Dorothea at the start has no way to reconcile her attraction to the beautiful with her Puritanic conceptions, and her respone to art is very crude. She "undergoes an education in the language of art, but she assimilates that language to a more encompassing experience of life", and turns to "a realist art implicated in its culture". Ladislaw teaches Dorothea the language of art through Ruskin, Goethe and Lessing, all of whom endorse a realism that governs the imagery and iconography of *Middlemarch*.

                                                              (ARTS)

340   Ringler, Ellin
        "*Middlemarch:* A Feminist Perspective", *Studies in the Novel,*
        15 (1983), 55–61

        Summarizes the predominantly negative responses of feminist
        critics to *Middlemarch* and argues that what should interest them
        is GE's depictions of female characters' "impressive personal
        dominance", her protests against the limits of education and
        opportunity faced by women, and her shrinking from the angry
        implications of her novel.

                                                          (FEMINISM)

341   Adams, Harriet Farwell
        "Dorothea and 'Miss Brooke' in *Middlemarch*", *Nineteenth-
        Century Fiction,* 39 (1984), 69–90

        An analysis of the relation of "Miss Brooke" to
        "Middlemarch". "Prelude" probably states the original theme,
        with emphasis on "martyrdom", recorded by GE long before.
        The novelistic turning-point in integrating the two stories is the
        famous turn to focus on Casaubon. "Middlemarch", with deep
        sources like "Miss Brooke", actually influenced the latter, but
        chapter 20 is the first true joining. The decision to connect the
        two was suggested by GE's reinterpretation of Dorothea's earlier
        preoccupation with religion. (See Beaty in 310).

342   Graver, Suzanne
        "Mill, *Middlemarch,* and Marriage", in Anne C. Hargrove and
        Maurine Magliocco (eds), PORTRAITS OF MARRIAGE IN
        LITERATURE (Western Illinois University Press, 1984), pp.
        55–65

        Juxtaposes Mill's *On the Subjection of Women* with
        Middlemarch and deals with GE's ambivalence about the
        woman question. GE's critique is very similar to Mill's. Lydgate
        can be taken as illustration of the kinds of marital disability that
        are seen by Mill to attest to the need for changing existing
        customs and practices. Dorothea and Casaubon takes the notion
        of woman as exalted helpmeet. The novel constantly puts in
        question the antagonistic notions of renunciation and freedom,
        one fostered by rhetoric, the other by plot, yet trying to do justice
        to both. Her analysis implies that the prevailing definitions of
        woman's nature were a construction of culture. Marriage
        dictated not reflected woman's nature.

343   McSweeney, Kerry
       MIDDLEMARCH (London: Allen and Unwin, 1984)

Part of the Unwin Critical Library, an Introduction meant less
for specialists than for students and as a handbook for teachers.
The book attempts to cover every aspect of the novel — sources,
biography, textual history, critical history — and to provide an
extensive critical analysis. The judgements are distinctly
Jamesian and often arbitrary. On the whole, this book is useful
in compiling materials and presenting commonsense analyses; it
must be warily engaged, however, because of the dogmatic and
authoritarian tendencies of its critical manner.

Daniel Deronda

(See also James in 46; Martin in 47; Zimmerman in 50)

344   Kaufman, David
"George Eliot and Judaism: An Attempt to Appreciate *Daniel Deronda*", translation of a three-part article in *Monatschrift für Geschichte und Wissenschaft* (1877)

345   Beebe, Maurice
"Visions are Creators: the Unity of *Daniel Deronda*", *Boston University Studies in English,* 1 (1955), 166–77

An early defence of the Deronda half of the novel. Beebe argues that *Daniel Deronda* is unified on an ideological, not narrative level, and traces GE's technique of dramatic opposition in the novel.

346   Thale, Jerome
"*Daniel Deronda:* The Darkened World", *Modern Fiction Studies,* 3 (1957), 119–26

Emphasizes what he considers a "new tone" in GE, particularly resulting from the confrontation with a new kind of evil, personified by Grandcourt but visible to some extent also in Gwendolen.

347   Carroll, David R.
"The Unity of *Daniel Deronda*", *Essays in Criticism,* 9 (1959), 369–80

Another treatment of the question of the two halves of the novel, in response to Leavis's condemnation of the Jewish half. Carroll maintains that *Daniel Deronda* possesses a structural unity by focusing on the effects of Gwendolen and Mordecai on Deronda.

348   Leavis, F.R.
"George Eliot's Zionist Novel", *Commentary,* 30 (1960), 317–25 (reprinted as "Introduction" to *Daniel Deronda* [New York: Harper Brothers, 1961])

Concedes that a serious reader must read the whole of the novel and cannot exclude the Deronda half, as he had suggested in 102. It is important then to understand how the Zionist part "fails to justify the place given it" in the total conception of the novel. The Jewish part "was done from the outside". There is an element of daydream in it, and Deronda himself is "very positively feminine". The failure is not intellectual but emotional.

349   Preyer, Robert
        "Beyond the Liberal Imagination: Vision and Unreality in *Daniel Deronda*", *Victorian Studies,* 4 (1960), 33–54

A consideration of "what went wrong" with the novel. Preyer rejects Leavis's charge of "immaturity", to argue that GE was trying to embody a different order of experience that was incompatible with the range of traditional realistic fiction. She sought to avoid a deterministic reading of the social pressures on individual action and turned to wisdom literature of mystics and visionaries. "We want to know why an urgent ethical concern with personal and social salvation . . . should lead a great master of reality into myth and fantasy". GE believed that she had to take into account powers and feelings that lay outside normal rational discourse or the realist techniques of fiction. *Daniel Deronda* "represents a final attempt to reconstitute the positive, creative side of the liberal humanist vision". The merely "literary" failure should not blind us to the importance and interest of this attempt.

350   Rosenberg, Edgar
        "The Jew as Hero and Isaiah Reborn", FROM SHYLOCK TO SVENGALI: JEWISH STEREOTYPES IN ENGLISH FICTION (Stanford: Stanford University Press, 1960), pp. 161–84

Very critical of GE's handling of Jewish matters in the novel. The Jews becomes mere "puppets", and GE's ideas come directly through them.

351   Robinson, Carole
        "The Severe Angel: A Study of *Daniel Deronda*", *English Literary History,* 31 (1964), 278–300

Except that GE needed a man for the political purposes of the novel, Daniel would have been a woman, like all his precursors. Daniel is "not a character but a compromise" and his ideas are falsely affirmed to be feelings. GE wants Deronda to be seen as a man of feeling, but she fails to "validate her claims". GE's explicit claims of fellow feeling work perniciously in the character of Deronda and in the novel as a whole; the "moral judgement is contradicted by its aesthetic judgement". Gwendolen is Daniel's moral, as well as aesthetic superior. "The ideology of sympathy and the contrast between 'social' and 'selfish' are the rocks upon which the novel founders".

352   Lerner, Laurence
       "The Education of Gwendolen Harleth", *Critical Quarterly*, 7
       (1965), 355–64

       Provides a well-argued but conventional reading, tracing Gwendolen's conversion from hardness, through suffering, to awakening, and juxtaposes it to the novel's weakness — the Jewish theme. GE's "not fully absorbed enthusiasm" gives way to "stiffness and melodrama".

353   Swann, Brian
       "Eyes in the Mirror: Imagery and Symbolism in *Daniel Deronda*", *Nineteenth-Century Fiction,* 23 (1969), 434–45

       A detailed reading of the images and metaphors of sight and eyes, and of glass and mirrors. These help explicate the meaning of Gwendolen's career.

354   Sudrann, Jean
       "*Daniel Deronda* and the Landscape of Exile", *English Literary History,* 37 (1970), 433–55

       The novel is an organically conceived experiment in which the double plot provides a modern definition of "isolation". From her own experience of the desolating "naked prose of the world", GE creates a modern wasteland landscape in which the self dissolves; the novel's struggles to reform identity entail major literary experiment. This is expressed through the double plot and melodramatic intrusions on the realistic surface. This sensitive analysis discusses the formation of images of alienation, dissolution and power on the surface of the action and their transformation into metaphors of the inner life. Melodrama gives "outward shape to inner drama".

355   Baker, William
"George Eliot's Readings in Nineteenth-Century Jewish Historians: A Note on the Background of *Daniel Deronda*", *Victorian Studies,* 15 (1972), 463–73

Baker shows that "the intellectual framework" for the views of the Jewish characters is developed from GE's reading of eight nineteenth-century Jewish historians. Much of the discussion at the Hand and Banner is traced with detailed analysis to sources in these historians.

356   Swann, Brian
"George Eliot and the Play: Symbol and Metaphor of the Drama in *Daniel Deronda*", *Dalhousie Review,* 52 (1972), 191–202

An examination of the dramatic terminology in the novel. Swann demonstrates how metaphors and symbols of the theatre are used to distinguish between two kinds of being, or ways of regarding the self. True drama is involvement with others as opposed to mere egotistical, theatrical performance.

357   Baker, William
"The Kabbalah, Mordecai, and George Eliot's Religion of Humanity", *Yearbook of English Studies,* 3 (1973), 216–21

A brief consideration of how GE's readings in the Kabbalah shaped her formulation of the relationship between Mordecai and Deronda.

358   Swann, Brian
"George Eliot's Ecumenical Jew, or, the Novel as Outdoor Temple", *Novel,* 8 (1974), 39–50

Sees the novel as expressive of the players' religious sensibilities. It represents a dream of reconciliations. The novel represents "all that is meaningful", to George Eliot.

359   Shalvi, Alice
         DANIEL DERONDA: A CENTENARY SYMPOSIUM
         (Jerusalem: Jerusalem Academic Press, 1976)

         Includes William Baker, "George Eliot and Zionism"; H.M.
         Daleski, "Owning and Disowning: the Unity of *Daniel
         Deronda*"; Baruch Hochman, "*Daniel Deronda:* The Zionist
         Plot and the Problematic of George Eliot's Art"; Laurence
         Lerner, "George Eliot's Struggle with Realism"; Alan Mintz,
         "Daniel Deronda and the Messianic Vocation"; Shmuel
         Werses, "The Jewish Reception of *Daniel Deronda*".

360   Witemeyer, Hugh
         "English and Italian Portraiture in *Daniel Deronda*",
         Nineteenth-Century Fiction, 30 (1976), 477–94

         Witemeyer demonstrates how each of the novel's two plots
         "incorporates a distinctive mode of literary portraiture": the
         English invoking the English portrait tradition, and the Jewish
         invoking the Italian. Witemeyer provides detailed background
         and illustrations to show how the stylistic contrast between
         portrait traditions mirrors moral contrasts.

                                                              (ARTS)

361   Wolfe, Thomas P.
         "The Inward Vocation: An Essay on George Eliot's *Daniel
         Deronda*", *Literary Monographs,* 8 (1976), 1–46

         Discusses the unevenness of *Daniel Deronda* as symptomatic of
         the conflicts in GE's moral and artistic conscience. Wolfe
         attempts a psychological explanation of why GE's insight into
         one form of unreality was linked to "unwitting indulgence of it
         in another form". The three sections of the monograph cover,
         first, "the terms of the 'egoistical' appeal to the reader", second,
         the connection between the two worlds of the novel, and third,
         the elaboration of the Gwendolen/Deronda contrast in GE's
         treatment of various artist figures in the novel.

362   Chase, Cynthia
         "The Decomposition of the Elephants: Double-Reading *Daniel
         Deronda*", *PMLA,* 93 (1978), 215–27

         Perhaps the best known deconstructionist reading of GE, this
         essay takes off from a letter from Hans Meyrick to Deronda. The

novel offers itself "not only as a history of the effects of causes but also as a story of 'the present causes of past effect'". The novel disguises its own rhetorical principles, the allusion to a "nonlinguistic fact or act". That fact is Deronda's circumcision (whose evasion is a condition for the narrative unfolding and the question of identity).

363   Howe, Irving
"George Eliot and the Jews", *Partisan Review,* 46 (1979), 359–75

The end of GE's career partly anticipates modernism. Understanding what GE was trying to do in her last novel will explain its "extraordinary interest" and is more valuable than worrying over its strengths and weaknesses. The problem of vocation, unresolved in *Middlemarch,* is urgent in *Daniel Deronda.* Her use of Judaism, against what she knew would be the public's dislike, was prompted by its revelation of English xenophobia, its evocation of her own youthful fervours, and its inspiration to imagination of the realization of moral ideals. GE's undertaking against the grain of Victorian culture was heroic. It is very much about power, which extends from the personal to the political, especially in the person of Grandcourt. To remain in society means becoming a Gwendolen, to achieve heroic ends, "society must be left behind".

364   Dale, Peter
"Symbolic Representation and the Means of Revolution in *Daniel Deronda*", *Victorian Newsletter,* 59 (Spring 1981), 25–30

Dale investigates GE's views of the philosophical status of symbols by considering *Daniel Deronda,* the "most symbolically self-conscious novel". At mid-career GE shifts from a positivist symbolism, which takes the reality of the natural world apart from mediating human consciousness, to phenomenological symbolism, which assumes that the world represented can never be known. In *Daniel Deronda* "the mind cannot perceive or comprehend existence except through the images of its own yearning". Dale analyses the famous duality of *Daniel Deronda* as GE's working out of a philosophical (and political) problem of her own in contemporary controversy, reflecting her rejection of positivism and alliance with Nietzsche and modernist thought on the power of language.

(PHILOSOPHY)

365   David, Deirdre
FICTIONS OF RESOLUTION IN THREE VICTORIAN
NOVELS: *NORTH AND SOUTH, OUR MUTUAL FRIEND,
DANIEL DERONDA* (New York: Columbia University Press,
1981), pp. 133–206

David studies the mediations between the social actuality novels
represent and the desires of their predominantly middle-class
readers that things not be as they are, *Daniel Deronda* fails to
reconcile "social and psychological realism and moral
correction, and Eliot's essentially middle-class . . . criticism".
GE, like Daniel, reads experience like a text, and "language is
ultimately insufficient in an effective transmission of social and
psychological actuality". Daniel and the novel as a whole
manifest distrust of working-class and Jewish life. "Eliot means
Gwendolen to be both heroine and metaphor" for imperialism,
social triviality, the sterility of upper-class life, and "collective
social guilt". In all details of the private story David interestingly
finds social reverberations.

366   Newton, K.M.
"*Daniel Deronda* and Circumcision", *Essays in Criticism,* 31
(1981), 313–27

Newton takes up the extraordinary subject of Daniel's
circumcision (discussed in Chase, 362, and Marcus, 126), as
evidence of GE's failure to engage adequately the Jewish theme.
Newton argues that its absence from the text is less striking than
its presence would be. The objectionable ease with which Daniel
accepts Mordecai's suggestion that he is a Jew can be accounted
for if his penis had already made the suggestion. The plot is
therefore reconcilable with realism.

367   Levine, Herbert
"The Marriage of Allegory and Realism in *Daniel Deronda*",
Genre, 15 (1982), 421–45

Considers "the problems of narrative disjunction" in the two
modes, "realism and allegory", which Levine says characterize
the novel. Emphasis on allegorical/religious aspects of the
narrative is useful, but claims that GE shows a belief in absolute
good and evil seem unproven. Levine argues that recognition of a
pervasive allegorical/mythical mode will allow a more coherent
sense of the novel.

368   Pell, Nancy
        "The Fathers' Daughters in *Daniel Deronda*", *Nineteenth-Century Fiction*, 36 (1982), 424–51

The novel explores the difficulties of the daughter in achieving cultural and social legitimacy within an unresponsive, if not actually menacing, patriarchal society. Uneasiness about the authority of the father and active resistance to it expand as GE attempts for the first time to integrate the critical perspectives of historical time and cultural distance with an intimate story of English country society. Finds interesting parallels of rejecting daughters in Catherine Arrowpoint and Charisi. Gwendolen, driven by the failure of "father", ends up marrying "the absolute incarnation of the illegitimate father". Yet in the end, Gwendolen wishes to restore the conventions of patriarchal power as atonement.

                                                        (FEMINISM)

369   Putzell-Korab, Sara M.
        "The Role of the Prophet: the Rationality of Daniel Deronda's Idealist Mission", *Nineteenth-Century Fiction*, 37 (1982), 170–87

In GE's attempt to find Daniel an identity through vocation, she is using an idealist tradition: "Eliot's sources for Mordecai's and . . . Daniel's vision identify them as rational idealists". The Jewish medieval sources are *Kuzari* by Halevi, and the Kabbalah. Analysing the relationship between Daniel and the Khazari, Putzell-Korab claims that for both the ideal and the rational come together in Judaism which provides "a rational ideal that unifies thought with act". Daniel's acts are also in relation to Mazzini's nationalism, and he is to be seen as an Hegelian, world-historical individual, a founder of states.

370   Moldstad, David
        "The Dantean Purgatorial Metaphor in *Daniel Deronda*", *Papers in Language and Literature*, 19 (1983), 183–98

In *Daniel Deronda*, GE draws on the *Divine Comedy* more than ever. The Dantean allusions form a large pattern, through accumulations of details. The marriage itself, for example, is purgatorial.

                                                        (COMPARISON)

371   Poole, Adrian
       "Hidden Affinities in *Daniel Deronda*", *Essays in Criticism,* 33
       (1983), 294–311

Concerned with the "allusions" in *Daniel Deronda,* where there
are more than in any other GE novel. Through allusion, GE
shows that all we are inheriting from the past are fragments,
"shreds and Patches". Gwendolen's story is strengthened by the
activity of allusion; Deronda's is weakened by its absence. But
allusions bind the two stories toegther and suggest "hidden
affinities". Poole ingeniously elaborates a web of
interconnectedness not only with Goethe and Shakespeare but
with classical myth — Ovid and Euripides, in particular. The
reading of allusions in three episodes becomes an unusually rich
and sensitive analysis of the novel.

372   Gallagher, Catherine
       "George Eliot and *Daniel Deronda,* The Prostitute and the
       Jewish Question", SEX, POLITICS AND SCIENCE IN THE
       NINETEENTH-CENTURY NOVEL, ed. Ruth Bernard
       Yeazell (Baltimore: The Johns Hopkins University Press, 1986),
       pp. 39–62

Supplements the metaphor of writer as father with that of
another tradition, writer as whore. Authorship is traditionally
allied to usury: "like money, the prostitute . . . is incapable of
natural procreation". "Language proliferates itself in a process
of exchange through the author". Gallagher uses the metaphor
to understand the ending of GE's career and of *Daniel Deronda.*
A complex and interesting analysis that connects the narrative
with the critique of commodity exchange, an affirmation of
cultural nationalism, and GE's assertion of her own identity as
writer and as woman.

"The Lifted Veil" and Other Stories

(See also 326, Beer)

373   Rubinstein, Elliot L.
       "A Forgotten Tale by George Eliot", *Nineteenth-Century Fiction,* 17 (1962), 175–83

       At a time when the story was less well known that it is today, Rubinstein described it and focused on the story's concentration on the mind of Latimer. He regards the scene as a waste land and as an extreme version of GE's treatment of thwarted desire, and the ending, with its Frankenstein-like experiment, as inadequately related to the rest of the story.

374   Hurley, Edward
       "'The Lifted Veil': George Eliot as Anti-Intellectual", *Studies in Short Fiction,* 5 (1968), 257–62

       The story demonstrates that full knowledge means alienation from human association. Mere intellectual powers must be accompanied by powers of love and sympathy. Latimer's accurate vision is of a world completely corrupt and venal and depraved.

375   Milner, Ian
       "George Eliot's Prague Story", *Prague Studies in English,* 15 (1973), 67–82

       Detects that in "The Lifted Veil", "motifs, images, and character situations are in purer form". These are important in shaping the structure of the mature novels. Retells the story and then focuses on Prague as a key motif. Compares the images to those of "The Waste Land", and the technique to that of Poe.

376   Swann, Charles
       "Déjà vu: Déjà lu: 'The Lifted Veil' as an Experiment in Art", *Literature and History,* 5 (1979), 40–57

       Noting the difference between the story and the rest of GE's work, Swann treats it as an experiment in art that allows her "to take a rather sideways look at some of the problems raised by determinism, and to do a critique of positivism". Latimer expresses many of the anxieties of GE as author, and the story dramatizes an "enquiry into the nature of artistic production and narrative method". The story is the only one of GE's works that actually deconstructs history and narrative as Hillis Miller claims she does in *Middlemarch* (see 123).

377   Gray, B.M.
"Pseudoscience and George Eliot's 'The Lifted Veil'", *Nineteenth-Century Fiction,* 36 (1982), 407–23

Finds the sources of "The Lifted Veil" in GE's correspondence with the phrenologist, George Combe, in 1852, which reveal GE's interest in mesmerism also. Latimer's story parallels the case of a clairvoyant patient of a Dr Gregory, described by Combe. Analysis of the story (and of its relations with that of another patient, Silas Marner) interestingly juxtaposes the "pseudoscientific" discourse of the time.

378   Eagleton, Terry
"Power and Knowledge in 'The Lifted Veil'", *Literature and History,* 9 (1983), 52–61

A consideration of the way disinterested knowledge is actually in the service of established class relations. For GE, the scientific necessity for transparency of the human subject contradicted the bourgeois mystification of the human subject. "All knowledge . . . contains a secret irony or incipient contradiction: it must at once master the object and confront it as other". Total omniscience obliterates the otherness and thus becomes solipsistic. Eagleton takes the story as a text for the confusion and contradictions of bourgeois society and its relation to knowledge.

379   Szirotny, J.S.
"Two Confectioners the Reverse of Sweet: The Role of Metaphor in Determining George Eliot's Use of Experience", *Studies in Short Fiction,* 21 (1984), 27–44

Metaphor shapes the experience GE used for her narratives. Szirotny locates the "experience" behind "Brother Jacob", and shows how it becomes metaphor. In the sketch of the Viennese model for David Faux and the story itself, the imagery of sweets is basic. Sweets come to symbolize greed, and for David the world becomes a set of sweet objects to be devoured. GE changes the real experience so that the confectioner is foiled, but in order "to deprive David of his prosperous trade through the agency of the brother he has wronged — she must both create Brother Jacob and found David's patronage on conditions that can change".

380   Viera, Carroll
"'The Lifted Veil' and George Eliot's Early Aesthetic", *Studies in English Literature,* 24 (1984), 749–67

Considers "The Lifted Veil" and GE's aesthetic theory, through comparison of the story to GE's earliest published writing, "Poetry and Prose from the Notebook of an Eccentric". There are striking parallels between the fictional figures, McCarthy, Adolphe, and Idone and Latimer. "Like the Romantics, George Eliot links heightened powers of perception to the intensity of experience and feeling, but she increasingly and emphatically also associates them with the attributes of sincerity and sympathy". "In Latimer GE provides her fullest exploration of the hypothesis that visionary powers may lead, not to sincerity and sympathy, but to disenchantment and creative impotence".

381   Dale, Peter Allan
"George Eliot's 'Brother Jacob': Fables and the Physiology of Common Life", *Philological Quarterly,* 64 (1985), 17–35

"Brother Jacob" is usefully read as an "exercise or experiment aimed at resolving certain philosophical-cum-aesthetic problems raised by *The Mill on the Floss*" — how to move "beyond the 'insane' world" that destroys Maggie. "Brother Jacob" "is the purest expression we have in GE's fiction of the ironist's perception . . . that people may, after all, be more ridiculous than they are lovable". Dale's analysis is extensive and complex and suggests a great deal about GE's views of the new commerce, of knowledge, and of the basis of human behaviour in the animal.

382   Gray, B.M.
Introduction to THE LIFTED VEIL (New York: Penguin Books/Virago Press, 1986)

Discusses the way the story deals with the relation between knowledge and human love, emphasizing the affirmation of the need of love with knowledge, of love before knowledge. Also points out the connection with phrenology and mesmerism.

Index of Subjects

Reference figures are to the item numbers in the text

Index of Contributors

Reference figures are to the item numbers in the text